FAMOUS WOMEN OF THE FRENCH COURT.

From the French of Imbert de Saint-Amand.

Each with Portrait, 12mo, $1.25.

Three Volumes on Marie Antoinette.

MARIE ANTOINETTE AND THE END OF THE OLD RÉGIME.
MARIE ANTOINETTE AT THE TUILERIES.
MARIE ANTOINETTE AND THE DOWNFALL OF ROYALTY.

Three Volumes on the Empress Josephine.

CITIZENESS BONAPARTE.
THE WIFE OF THE FIRST CONSUL.
THE COURT OF THE EMPRESS JOSEPHINE.

Four Volumes on the Empress Marie Louise.

THE HAPPY DAYS OF MARIE LOUISE.
MARIE LOUISE AND THE DECADENCE OF THE EMPIRE.
MARIE LOUISE AND THE INVASION OF 1814.
MARIE LOUISE, THE RETURN FROM ELBA AND THE HUNDRED DAYS.

MARIE ANTOINETTE AND HER THREE CHILDREN.

Marie Antoinette

AT THE TUILERIES

1789-1791

BY

IMBERT DE SAINT-AMAND

TRANSLATED BY

ELIZABETH GILBERT MARTIN

WITH PORTRAIT

WILDSIDE PRESS

CONTENTS.

—◦◦◦—

FIRST PART.

SECOND PART.

THE VARENNES JOURNEY.

iii

THIRD PART.

THE CLOSE OF 1791.

Marie Antoinette

AT THE TUILERIES

1789-1791

FIRST PART.

I.

THE INSTALLATION AT THE TUILERIES.

THE drama of the Tuileries begins. It is the sixth of October, 1789. The hour is ten in the evening. After a day of indescribable suffering, the royal family, who left Versailles at one in the afternoon, had entered the Hôtel de Ville at Paris toward nine o'clock. "It is always with pleasure and with confidence," Louis XVI. had said, "that I find myself amidst the inhabitants of my good city of Paris." In repeating the King's discourse, the mayor, Bailly, had forgotten the words "with confidence." The Queen instantly recalled them. "Gentlemen," went on Bailly, "you are more fortunate than if I had said it myself." Then Louis XVI. and his family returned to the Tuileries. It was not without hesitation and sadness that they entered. The palace seemed all the more sombre by reason of the contrast between its black façade and the illuminations in the neighboring streets. Uninhabited since the majority of Louis XV., it was gloomy, out of

1

repair, unfurnished, and undecorated. The locks closed badly. The aspect was bleak, disastrous.

On the morning of October 7 the Queen awakes in the Tuileries. What things had happened, what tragedies, what emotions within twenty-four hours! Is it a nightmare? Is it reality? Yesterday it was still the city of the Sun-King, the splendid palace of Versailles. This morning it is the Tuileries, forbidding as a prison. What formidable cries are these, whose menacing echoes are still resounding in the sovereign's ears? What are these lugubrious and bloody sights which she cannot banish from her eyes, — the bands of pikemen, the hideous prostitutes of the galleries of the Palais Royal, the infernal viragoes of the Revolution, the livid heads of the hapless, decapitated body-guards? Will these cries of hatred and assassination, these oaths, these blasphemies, these insults, cease at last? Those reports of musketry, that storm of invectives and ferocious jests — can it be that they will not begin anew? This residence where Marie Antoinette, after a short and unquiet slumber, re-opens her eyes to the light — is it a palace or a dungeon? What men are these who stand about the royal chamber? Are they servants, or jailers, or assassins? These ragged women who crowd beneath the windows — what are they going to say? what are they going to do? Will they force the chamber doors to-day as they did yesterday, and riddle with pike and sabre thrusts the bed of the Queen of

France, the daughter of Maria Theresa? What has befallen her? What can the future have in store? What may be hoped? what feared? How shall she hide the sentiments of indignation and sacred anger, which burst from a noble heart? What figure can she make in presence of this riotous upheaval? How support the supreme humiliations which strike at the lineage of Saint Louis, of Henri IV., and Louis XIV.? The atmosphere is overcharged with storms. Doom weighs heavily on this sinister palace which, alas! was to be merely the vestibule of the scaffold. Marie Antoinette feels herself surrounded by furies. One might say that from every window, from every side of the wall, from behind each piece of furniture, poniards were aimed at the august victim. The most intrepid woman would tremble. Oh! what a morning! what an awakening!

And yet the rays of hope were here and there to shine through this overclouded sky. The presence of the King and his family in the capital produced a certain cessation of the storm. The bakers' shops were no longer besieged; there was sufficient food. The people thronged towards the Tuileries. The avenues, the courtyards, the gardens, were encumbered by the crowd. In the morning of October 7, the same women, who, astride the cannons, had yesterday surrounded the carriage of the captive royal family with threats and insults, came underneath the Queen's windows, demanding to present their homage. Marie Antoinette showed herself to the crowd. As her bonnet partially shaded her face, she was besought to remove it, that she might be better seen. She granted the request. Royalty was no longer more than a plaything, with which the people amused themselves before breaking it. The women who yesterday hung on to the steps of the royal carriage, clung fast to its doors, and leaned over Marie Antoinette, trying to touch her, to soil her with their breath, were now in parley with her.

"Send away from you," said one, "all these courtiers who ruin kings. Love the inhabitants of your good city."

"I loved them at Versailles," replied the Queen; "I will love them just the same at Paris."

"Yes, yes," said another; "but on the fourteenth of July you wanted to besiege the city and have it bombarded."

"You were told so," answered the Queen, "and you believed it. It was that which caused the woes of the people and of the best of kings."

A third woman addressed the sovereign in German.

"German!" said Marie Antoinette; "I no longer understand it. I have become so thorough a Frenchwoman that I have even forgotten my mothertongue."

There was a burst of applause. The women asked the Queen for the flowers and ribbons on her bonnet. She unfastened them herself and gave them away. The throng cried, "Long live our good Queen!"

While the courtyards and the garden of the Tuileries were resounding with cheers, the body-guards, pale, drooping, and bearing still the marks of the distress they had endured the previous evening, were making the rounds of the public promenades, under the escort of the National Guards, yesterday their victors, to-day their comrades. They were received with sympathy on all sides. One would have said the reconciliation was complete.

Throughout the day numberless deputations visited the King. Louis XVI., always an optimist, seemed to have forgotten totally the violence of the day before. His courtiers were far from sharing his serenity. Etiquette was still maintained, but the gentlemen attached to his service fulfilled their duties sadly. The perpetual supervision of M. de Lafayette; the presence of the National Guards, those soldiers of the Revolution; the absence of the body-guards, those soldiers of fidelity; the invasion of the sanctuary of monarchy by a crowd of enemies or intruders; the gradual diminution of the state indispensable to the prestige of royalty; the sadness of that fair and good Queen whose eyes were reddened by incessant tears; the progress of the revolutionary movement which menaced the liberty, the possessions, and the life of the French nobility, — all this struck unfeigned consternation to the hearts of the King's attendants.

Many had already emigrated; but, on the other hand, there was one woman who, at the first mention of danger, had hastened to the post of honor and devotion. It was the Princess de Lamballe. At nine in the evening of October 7 she was sitting tranquilly with her father-in-law, the Duke de Penthièvre, in the castle of Eu, when a courier arrived at full speed, bringing the news of what had passed at Versailles during the last two days. " O papa," cried the Princess, " what horrible events! I must go at once." At midnight, in frightful weather and profound darkness, Madame de Lamballe left the castle of Eu, to repair in all haste to the Queen at Paris. She arrived there during the night of October 8, and took up her quarters on the ground-floor of the Pavilion of Flora. In her capacity as superintendent, she gave several soirées there, at some of which Marie Antoinette made her appearance. But as the Queen speedily became convinced that her position no longer permitted her attendance at large receptions, she remained in her own apartments, reading, praying, sewing, and supervising the education of her children.

Madame Elisabeth wrote to the Abbé de Lubersac on October 16: " The Queen, who has had incredible courage, begins to be in better favor with the people. I hope that in time, and by unremitting prudence, we may regain the love of the Parisians, who have merely been deceived. But, sir, the people of Versailles! Have you ever seen more frightful ingratitude? No; I think that Heaven in wrath peopled that city with monsters out of hell. How long it will take to make them recognize their injustice!

And if I were king, how long it would take me to
believe in their repentance! What ingrates toward
an honest man! Would you believe, sir, that all our
misfortunes, far from bringing me back to God, give
me a veritable disgust for all that relates to prayer?
Beg of Heaven for me the grace not to abandon
everything. . . . Ask also that the reverses of France
may recall to a better mind those who have contributed to them by their irreligion."

During several days people continued to obstruct
the courtyards of the Tuileries.• Their indiscretion
was carried to such a point that several market-
women ventured to climb into the apartment of Madame Elisabeth, who had rooms on the ground-floor
of the Pavilion of Flora, on the side next the courtyard. The Princess was obliged to quit this apartment, and install herself on the first floor, in order
to be sheltered from importunate glances and the
invasions of the fishwomen.

People who had been hired by the party of disorder came every instant to make outrageous and indecent remarks beneath the windows of the chateau.
The revolutionists, in order to insult more deeply
the majesty of the crown, sent men belonging to the
dregs of the people to the King himself, under the
title of delegates. The abuse was so great, that one
of the Ministers proposed to forbid the entrance of
such deputations into the palace. "No," said the
unfortunate monarch; "they may present themselves; we shall have courage to listen to them."

One day when these pretended delegates were ha-
ranguing Louis XVI., one of them dared to accuse
the Queen, who was present, in most offensive terms.
" You mistake," said the King, gently; " the Queen
and I have not the intentions with which we are cred-
ited. We act in concert for your common welfare."
When the deputation retired, Marie Antoinette fell
to weeping.

Augeard, her private secretary, gives an account in
his very curious Memoirs, of a conversation he had with
her soon after the days of October: " Your Majesty
is a prisoner." — " My God! what are you saying to
me?" " Madame, it is most true. From the time
when Your Majesty ceased to have a guard of honor,
you were a prisoner." — " These men here, I contend,
are more attentive than our guards." " The attention of jailers. I will offer you no other proof of it,
Madame, than to remind you of the precaution you
have taken to see whether any one is listening at the
doors. Would you have taken it with your guards?"
— "But what must be done, then?"

Augeard advised the Queen to rejoin her brother,
the Emperor. He added: " I know only one way —
but that is infallible — to save the King, yourself,
your children, and all France. It is for you to go
away with Madame Royale and the Dauphin, dressing him as a little girl, and go as a private person, —
not as a queen or a princess. You could no longer
be set up in opposition to the new Constitution they
want to give us, and your lives would be safe."

Augeard went on to develop a complete plan of escape. The Queen, with her children, and Madame Thibaut, her maid, were to go upon the roof, and descend from there by a flight of stairs which led to the Court of the Princes. She was to depart by way of this court, leaving at the Tuileries a letter expressed in some such words as these: —

"MY MOST HONORED LORD AND AUGUST SPOUSE: After the attempts to assassinate me on the fifth and sixth of this month, I cannot conceal from myself that I have the frightful misfortune to displease my subjects. They imagine that I am opposed to the new Constitution they desire to give to your realm. In order to banish every shadow of suspicion which relates to me, I prefer to condemn myself to profound retreat outside of your dominions, which I shall not re-enter, my most honored and august spouse, until the Constitution shall have been established."

This letter would be delivered to the King at his rising, the Queen having departed the night before.

"No, no; I will not go away!" cried Marie Antoinette. "My duty is to die at the King's feet." The Queen was right. She remained courageously at the post of devotion and danger. Those who sought to persuade her to abandon her husband gave counsel unworthy of her lofty heart. By following such advice the daughter of the great Maria Theresa might have saved her life, but she would have lost something more desirable — her honor.

II.

THE monarchy, although shaken, still had tradition and memory on its side. As yet no one spoke of a republic; and the future regicides, the Marats and the Robespierres themselves, were still royalists by conviction. Louis XVI. could not bring himself to believe that the nation was being estranged from him. The cheers with which he was greeted when he passed by nourished fatal illusions in his mind; and the ceremonious visit paid him by the National Assembly on October 20, 1789, increased the serene assurance which Marie Antoinette did not share, and to which he was to fall a victim.

As soon as he arrived in Paris, he had written to the Assembly: —

"GENTLEMEN: The affection displayed toward me by the inhabitants of my good city of Paris, and the urgency of the Commune, have decided me to make it my most habitual place of residence. As I am confident that you will be unwilling to separate from me, I desire that you should appoint commissioners to seek the most convenient location for you here.

10

I will at once give orders to have it got in readiness. Thus, without relaxing your useful labors, I shall render more prompt and easy the communications which mutual confidence makes increasingly necessary."

Provisional choice was made of the great hall of the archbishop's palace. The Assembly sat there for the first time on October 20, and decided to wait on the King in a body. The visit took place at six o'clock the same evening.

Etiquette was still maintained, and a resemblance between the apartments of the Tuileries and those of Versailles was soon established. There was a salon, which they called the Œil-de-Bœuf, and the Gallery of Diana was devoted to the same purposes as had been the Gallery of the Mirrors. A person in the Carrousel, opposite the chateau, could see in front of him three courtyards, separated from each other by walls seven or eight feet high: on the left the Court of the Princes; in the middle the Royal Court, which led to the Central Pavilion; and on the right the Swiss Court, leading to the Pavilion of Marsan. Those who came to visit the King entered by the Royal Court. On the right-hand side of the vestibule of the Central Pavilion was a large and handsome staircase. On its first landing, and also on the right, was the chapel, which was very simple; the sacristy was behind the altar, above which was the gallery for the musicians, opposite that of the King and Queen. At this landing the staircase divided

into two symmetrical parts; that on the left conduct-
ing to the hall called the Hundred Switzers, the
great hall from which could be seen both the court
and the garden, and which rose to the roof of the
Central Pavilion; it was afterwards the Hall of the
Marshals. The King's apartment included, besides
this hall, the following rooms: the Hall of the
Guards, afterwards the Salon of the First Consul;
the royal ante-chamber, also called the Œil-de-Bœuf
and later the Hall of Apollo; the bedchamber (a
state chamber afterwards called the Throne Room);
the great royal cabinet (where the Council of the
Ministry sat, and known afterwards as the Salon of
Louis XIV.); and finally the Gallery of Diana, called
also the Ambassadors' Gallery.

At six in the evening the members of the National
Assembly met in the Tuileries in the royal ante-
chamber (the Hall of Apollo). No distinctions of
rank were observed, and, for the first time, the deputies attended a royal audience without being in court
dress. Was not this a sign of the times? The ushers
opened the two doors by which entrance is made into
the bedchamber (the future Throne Room). The
masters of ceremonies, walking on either hand of
the President, introduced the Assembly. The King
received them, seated in an armchair. He removed
his hat only during their entrance and while receiving the salutations of the President, M. Fréteau, a
member of Parliament who, in spite of his advanced
opinions, was to perish on the scaffold like the King

himself. M. Fréteau made a speech in which the following remarks occur: "The affection of the French people for their monarch seemed incapable of increase after that memorable day when their voice proclaimed you the restorer of liberty. There remained, Sire, a still more touching title to be given you, — that of the nation's best friend. Henri IV. received it from the inhabitants of a city in which he spent his youth. Historical monuments apprise us that in the letters he wrote them he signed himself 'Your best friend.' This title, Sire, is due to you from the whole of France. We have seen Your Majesty, calm in the midst of tumults, taking on yourself all risks and seeking to withdraw your excited people from them by your presence and your solicitous care; we have seen you renouncing your pleasures, your recreations, and your tastes, in order to come among a turbulent multitude and announce the return of peace, to strengthen the bonds of concord, and rally the exhausted forces of this vast empire. How sweet it is to us, Sire, to gather into one the benedictions with which an immense people surround you, and offer them in honorable tribute. We add to them the assurance of a zeal continually more active in the maintenance of law and the defence of your protecting authority."

The King was not prepared for this visit from the National Assembly.

"Gentlemen," he replied with emotion, "I am

content with the attachment you express for me. I counted on it. I receive the testimony of it with profound feeling."

The Assembly then expressed a desire to present their respects to the Queen. The King permitted all the deputies to pass through his cabinet (the Salon of Louis XIV.) in order to arrive at Marie Antoinette's apartments by the Gallery of Diana. The ushers opened the two leaves of the folding-door which leads from the bedchamber to the Royal Cabinet, and the deputies passed through, bowing very low to Louis XVI., who had placed himself near this door.

At the end of the Gallery of Diana, on the right-hand side, ended a staircase which led from the ground-floor to the first story and the rooms formerly occupied by the wife of Louis XIV., and called the Queen's Apartments. They are five in all, looking down upon the garden, and with the Gallery of Diana just behind them. Here Marie Antoinette received the visit of the Assembly. The Queen, who had not been forewarned of their arrival, was at the moment at her toilet, getting ready to play in public. A desire not to keep the deputies waiting decided her to give them an immediate audience without putting on more ceremonious attire. She seated herself in an armchair in the principal room, and the Assembly were presented by the masters of ceremonies as had been the case with the King. One of them, M. de Nantouillet, who published an

account of this visit, remarks that the Queen, accustomed to receive the constituted bodies in the same
manner as the King, need not have risen at the
entrance of the Assembly, and that in doing so, and
in saying a word concerning the fact that she was
not in full dress, she wished to give them a special
mark of her esteem.

"Madame," said the President, "the first desire of
the National Assembly on arriving in the capital was
to present the King with the tribute of their respect
and love. They could not resist the natural opportunity to offer you also their good wishes. Receive
them, Madame, such as we form them, lively, ardent,
and sincere. It would be a real satisfaction if the
National Assembly might behold in your arms that
illustrious child, the offspring of so many kings tenderly cherished by their people, — the descendant of
Louis IX., of Henri IV., of him whose virtues are
the hope of France. Neither he nor the authors of
his life will ever enjoy so much prosperity as we
desire for them."

The Queen replied: " I am touched, as I ought to
be, with the sentiments expressed toward me by the
National Assembly. If I had been notified of their
intention, they would have been received in a more
befitting manner." Then Marie Antoinette commanded the Master of Ceremonies to go and find the
Dauphin. As soon as the child was brought, she took
him in her arms, and showed him to all the deputies.
Cries of "Long live the King!" "Long live the

Queen!" "Long live Monseigneur the Dauphin!"
resounded with enthusiasm. For a moment Marie
Antoinette was distracted from the thought of her
afflictions.

A few days later she changed her quarters, and,
leaving the first story, installed herself on the ground-
floor, where she had her dressing-room, her bedchamber, and her salon. As to Louis XVI., he continued
to live in the apartment which, since the reign of
Louis XIV., had been called the "apartment of the
King." It communicated with the Great Cabinet (the
Salon of Louis XIV.), and comprised three rooms,
looking on the garden, — a small cabinet intended for
the first valet de chambre, the sovereign's bedchamber, and a library. Louis XVI. had his son and
daughter placed near him in the apartment known as
"the apartment of the Queen," which Marie Antoinette had just vacated for another on the ground-
floor. In addition to his rooms in the first story, he
occupied three on the ground-floor, which were situated in the angle of the intermediate pavilion, between those of Flora and the Centre, one of which
communicated with the Queen's dressing-room.
Every morning, having spent the first moments
after rising in devotional exercises, he descended to
his little apartment on the ground-floor by a narrow
private staircase. He looked first at his thermome-
ter, and then received the greetings of his wife and
children. It was there also that he breakfasted,
served by one domestic only, the Queen taking ad-

vantage of this moment to come and chat with her husband. From there, too, he could examine what was going on in the garden without being seen, and listen to the remarks made just under his windows.

In spite of everything, the unfortunate monarch still preserved the greatest illusions. Such manifestations as that just made by the National Assembly deceived him concerning the extreme gravity of the situation. He believed that he was still loved and respected. Even the October days had not cured him of his fallacious optimism. Doubtless, the monarchy had not entirely lost its prestige, and the National Assembly were sincere when they expressed sentiments of fidelity toward their King. But the Revolution made incessant progress. As was remarked by Madame de Béarn, the daughter of the governess of the royal children, it was like one of those great currents which carry away even vessels which seek to cast anchor.

III.

WHAT a varied spectacle! What a tragi-comedy! What diverse figures! What contradictory emotions! What an amalgam of ideas and passions, of vices and virtues! Here, marquises and dukes; there, people of the faubourgs and insurgents. Red heels here; red bonnets there. Here, the language of courts; there, the insults of the market-place. In the Tuileries, elegance still, and politeness, and the chivalrous manners of the old régime; and a stone's throw distant, in the pestilent streets neighboring the Carrousel, the threats and hatred of a populace in rags; a little beyond, in the galleries of the Palais Royal, speech-making agitators, and the prostitutes who played such leading parts in the October days; beside the garden of the Tuileries, the riding-school where the National Assembly has its noisy sessions, its bitter discussions, and the stormy eloquence of its Mirabeau, the thunderer; on every street, in every square, colporteurs shouting forth their lies, newsmongers, Paul Prys, gossips who delight in calumny and the unhealthy emotions of sedition,

18

who play at being soldiers in the National Guards,
at politics in the cafés, at demagogy in the clubs,
mischief-makers who amuse themselves by rekind-
ling everywhere badly extinguished firebrands; in
the outskirts of Paris the principal soldiers of the
insurrection, the future Septembrists, the future
furies of the guillotine. What blows! What shocks!
This old régime which is dead — this new régime
which is still unborn! What a chaos! What seeth-
ing in this alembic, this furnace! What throes, what
anguish, what rending, is not France to endure, that
she may bring forth, in suffering, modern society,
her daughter! What electricity in the air! What
ensanguined or sombre clouds on the horizon! What
a vast hubbub of confused and noisy sounds, — beating of drums, applause and yells of disapproval in
the Assembly and the clubs, the ringing of bells, the
stroke of the tocsin! Paris is disturbed, tumultuous,
full of inflammable materials. One would say the
ground is mined. At every step one dreads a sudden
explosion. The soil is volcanic. One sees everything as if through the glare of a conflagration.

The Revolution is everywhere. Even in the salons
of the Faubourg Saint-Germain there is a left and
a right who dispute as bitterly as they do in the
National Assembly. Farewell that Attic wit, that
sweetness, that urbanity, which for so long have made
Parisian salons veritable schools of good taste and
grace! Unpleasant politics have become the only
topic of conversation. Everybody talks loud and

listens very little. Ill humor pierces through the
tone as through the glance. The women lose most
by this change in the manners of good society. It is
only the gentle passions which befit their features,
their voices, the delicacy of their entire being, and
behold them railing like demoniacs! Politics dis-
figures them, and anger makes them ugly.

At the theatre things are still worse than in the
salons. The play-houses are transformed into tilt-
yards where the combatants give themselves over to
perpetual contests. Whenever a favorable allusion
permits the royalists to display their sentiments
toward the King and Queen, they consider it a great
triumph to drown the actor's voice by noisy applause.
Then they hasten to the palace to say that public
opinion is coming round to good sense, and the revolutionists are crushed. But the Jacobins come in
force to the next play. They insult the aristocrats.
They cheer enthusiastically every line which breathes
of liberty ; they hiss furiously all those which might
recall the love of the people for their kings.

At the Théâtre Français, when *Charles Ninth* is
played, look at the public, a more curious spectacle
than the stage. At the end of the fourth act, when
the dismal bell announces the moment of the massa-
cre, do you see him who listens to it with a dull
groan? Do you hear him who cries, "Silence !
silence !" as if he feared lest the strokes of this
death bell should not resound loud enough within
his heart, where they feed the sensations of vengeance and of hatred?

And, in the midst of all this, sentimental phrases, pictures in the style of Greuze, a humanitarian, philosophic jargon borrowed from Jean-Jacques Rousseau, a sort of patriotic festival, an orgy of false fraternity. French gaiety, too, which does not lose its rights, irony which blends with enthusiasm, gross puns succeeding to the accents of eloquence, juggler's clowns who chatter while Mirabeau is speaking, laughter and tears, the grotesque and the sublime. At the side of noble enthusiasms and generous ideas, mean and wretched passions, envious women, many of whom rejoice to see the Queen unhappy; the levelling sentiment which finds pleasure in the decay and humiliation of the court and the aristocracy; the great capital in a shudder; the theatres always full; the churches still thronged with the faithful, who seek by their prayers to turn away the wrath of God; optimists who, in the triumphant age of iron, persist in predicting the age of gold; pessimists whose most sinister previsions are outdone by events; in fine, beyond all this vehement crowd whose cries and murmurs are like the tumult of the waves, a few sages, troubled but silent, who ask themselves how all this will end, and, as from a mountain top, look down at the vessels tossing upon the billows.

What is most striking in the scene presented by Paris at the close of 1789, is its extreme variety. Count de Ségur, coming back from his embassy to Saint Petersburg, shows us the different aspects presented by the capital in a single day.

In the morning he goes to see Baron de Besenval, who is shut up in the prison of the Châtelet for having resisted the riot when commanding the troops of the Parisian garrison at the beginning of the Revolution. An immense crowd assembled on the quay obstructs the thoroughfare in spite of the efforts of the National Guard, and fills the air with vociferations. Some madmen, accusing the judges of delay and the authorities of treason, are shouting loudly for the prisoner's head. It takes M. de Ségur a long time to arrive, and gives him great trouble to make his way through this furious multitude. Reaching the prison at last, he enters by a wicket under a low door. He passes with repugnance through the gloomy windings of this den of vice and crime; after he has mounted the tower stairs, he enters a tolerably clean chamber, where he sees Baron de Besenval, not merely calm and courageous, but with his accustomed gaiety, talking with several friends and some women, as amiable as they are charming, who have come to make his captivity more agreeable.

An hour later, M. de Ségur is on the Place de Grève. There he sees many assemblages which the National Guard is painfully trying to disperse. From there he goes to the market, where he has before him a great public mart in full activity, as in the midst of the profoundest peace. Then he goes to the Palais Royal. He enters that famous garden, the centre of industry, the focus of corruption, an arena always open to the seditious, who make it the rendezvous of their machinations. A curious crowd are surrounding a man who, mounted on a table, is declaiming vehemently against the perfidy of the court, the pride of the nobles, the cupidity of the rich, the inertia of the legislators, and who concludes, applauded by some and criticised by others, by proposing incendiary motions.

Disgusted by this scene, Count de Ségur goes away and enters the garden of the Tuileries. The weather is splendid. The terrace and the alleys are filled with peaceful promenaders. The prettiest women of Paris are displaying their dresses and their charms. Satisfaction beams on every face. One would think it was a holiday.

M. de Ségur leaves the Tuileries and goes through the Champs Élysées, where all is confusion. He sees a multitude of armed men. They are old soldiers of the French Guard, who, to execute a projected revolt, are going to the great square, the appointed place for their reunion; but Lafayette, warned of their gathering, hastens with several battalions of the National Guard, and disarms them.

In the evening, to banish the souvenirs of the day, M. de Ségur goes to the Opera. This time he is tempted to imagine, that, up to now, he has been dreaming. Who would not believe himself to be living in the happiest and most peaceful of epochs? Behold this affluence of spectators, this charming ballet, these magnificent decorations; recognize in the boxes the most distinguished people of the court and of the city. Look at these fashionable women,

who glance from behind the fans they manage so
well. Listen to this enchanting music, which ban-
ishes anxiety and care. What an opening in the
cloudy sky! Over the volcano, around the crater,
whence flames and lava are about to pour, there are
still greensward, fields, and flowers.

In the tableau of Paris, at the close of 1789, the
court does not occupy a brilliant place. One might
say that royalty, doubtful of itself, is effacing itself
voluntarily, and dwindling away. Every day it loses
a little more of its prestige. The rays of the royal
sun, once so dazzling, are growing pale. "One would
not suspect that there is a court at Paris. All is
absolutely quiet. There is no question of hunts or
balls, of comedies or of concerts. Economy looks
like hoarding, and certainly Voltaire would not say
to-day (December 10, 1789), '*How proud Paris is of
the court of Louis.*'" [1]

However, there are still cards on Sundays, dinners
in public on Tuesdays and Thursdays, and all the
nobility of Paris repair assiduously to the chateau.
There are even many persons who would not have
dared to pretend to present themselves at court the
year before, but who now, under pretext of zeal for
the royal cause, are seeking to become intimate at
the Tuileries. But events have stamped the palace
with a character of profound sadness. Its faded

---

[1] *Secret Correspondence concerning Louis XVI. and Marie
Antoinette.* MS. of the Imperial Library of Saint Petersburg, published by M. de Lescure. 2 vols. Plon.

tapestries, its arches damaged by the weather, its
dilapidated aspect, give it, on the whole, the air of
an assemblage of things, once brilliant, but now
mouldy, which recall both the grandeur and the
decadence of the monarchy. The royal family is
free to walk in the garden only at certain hours.
Then the public is excluded. Some of the soldiers
say vulgarly that the King is "let out." And yet,
shaken as it is, royalty, with an abler monarch,
would still have great resources. Betrayed by itself,
rather than by the feebleness and incapacity of its
defenders, it still sustains itself, and Louis XVI.
needs three years more to consummate a downfall
wrought chiefly by himself.

IV.

THE EXECUTION OF THE MARQUIS DE FAVRAS.

THE hour was approaching when Louis XVI. would see every prerogative of royalty torn from him, even the right to pardon. Already, in the early months of 1790, he dared not save from death a royalist whose crime had been an excess of monarchical zeal. The gibbet of the Marquis de Favras was the prelude to the King's scaffold.

M. de Favras was born in 1745. He served in the army with distinction, and his wife was a daughter of the Prince of Anhalt-Schauenburg. Ever since the Revolution began he had been considering one project after another for rescuing the monarchy from the dangers surrounding it. His naturally vivid imagination became overheated, and he looked on himself with great simplicity as the future saviour of the throne. His plan was to carry off the King, and take him to Péronne, and to arrest Lafayette and Necker. It was claimed that he also wished to assemble twelve thousand cavalry in Paris, and support them by an army of twenty thousand Swiss, twenty thousand Sardinians, and twelve thousand

26

Germans; but this was not proved. M. de Favras communicated his ideas to a number of the persons surrounding Monsieur, the King's brother, but no one attached serious importance to them. He was then imprudent enough to try to sound certain officers of the National Guard, who, instead of receiving him favorably, informed against him. He was at once arrested, and sent to the Châtelet to be tried. As the name of Monsieur had been implicated in the denunciation, the Prince went at once to the Paris Commune in order to counteract, without a moment's delay, the suspicious rumors which might get into circulation. "From the day," said he, "when in the Second Assembly of Notables I declared myself concerning the fundamental questions which divide men's minds, I have not ceased to believe that a great revolution is impending; that the King, by virtue of his intentions, his virtues, and his supreme rank, ought to be at the head of it, since it cannot be advantageous to the nation without being equally so to the monarch; and, finally, that royal authority should be the rampart of national liberty, and national liberty the basis of royal authority." This discourse was received with general applause, and the Prince was accompanied by the crowd back to the Luxembourg palace, where he resided.

As for the unfortunate Favras, everybody was bitter against him. During the whole of the trial the people kept up an incessant threatening of the judges and the cry, "To the lamp-post with him!" It was even necessary to have pieces of artillery and numerous troops constantly drawn up in the courtyard of the Châtelet. The crowd had been exasperated by the acquittal of Baron de Besenval and others implicated in the affairs of July 14. It is claimed that Lafayette said: "If M. de Favras is not condemned, I will not answer for the National Guard." The principal charge against the accused was a letter from M. de Foucault, who asked him: "Where are your troops? From what direction will they enter Paris? I would like to serve among them." This was sufficiently vague, and no trace was discovered either of the cavaliers who were to make the supposed attack, or of the Swiss, German, and Piedmontese armies expected to aid them. Nevertheless, M. de Favras was condemned to death. He listened to his sentence with the greatest calmness. "I pity you exceedingly," said he to the judges, "if the simple testimony of two men is enough to make you condemn an innocent person." He was hanged in the Place de Grève on February 19, 1790. As soon as the people saw him in the cart with the rope around his neck, and the hangman behind him, they broke into wild exultation and cries of enthusiastic joy. It was night, and lamps were lighted all over the Place de Grève. They even put one on the gibbet. "Citizens," cried the condemned, "I die innocent: pray God for me." Then, turning to the hangman, he said, "Come, my friend, do your duty." The crowd responded with ironical clapping of the hands, ferocious laughter,

and repeated cries of "Skip, Marquis!" As soon as
he was hanged, a number of voices cried, "*Encore!*"
as if to demand more executions. The people wanted
to get at the dead body, tear it in pieces, and carry
the bleeding head on the end of a pike. The
National Guard succeeded in preventing this scene,
worthy of cannibals, but only with great difficulty
and at the point of the bayonet.

Madame Elisabeth wrote next day to the Marquise
de Bombelles: "My head and heart are so full of
yesterday that it is hardly possible for me to think of
anything else. I hope that his blood may not fall
back upon his judges. But nobody (except the people and that class of beings whom one cannot call
men because it would lower humanity) understands
for what he was condemned. He was so imprudent
as to wish to serve his king. Behold his crime. I
hope that this unjust execution may have the effect
of persecutions, and that from his ashes men who
still love their country may spring up again to
avenge her on the traitors by whom she is deceived.
I hope, also, that Heaven, for the sake of the courage
he showed during the four hours at the Hôtel de
Ville before his execution, may have pardoned his
sins. Pray for him, my heart; you cannot perform
a better work."

The execution of M. de Favras had become a fixed
idea with Madame Elisabeth. On February 23 she
wrote again to Madame de Bombelles: "Heavens,
Bombe, how angry your letter made me! I own

that I was extremely wrong. But no matter, I must
tell you why. I was penetrated by the injustice of
M. de Favras's death, by the superb way in which he
ended his life, and the love he showed for his king
(which was the sole cause of his death). For two
days I had been thinking of nothing else; my heart,
my soul, my entire being was filled with nothing
but this idea, and then I receive a letter in which
you say to me, ' But what was the wretched man
thinking about?' You may judge whether your
princess, who does not always give herself time for
reflection, fell into a rage against poor Bombe, who,
nevertheless, had done nothing, and who, if she had
been here, would have wondered, like all who breathe
in Paris, both at the injustice of his death and the
courage with which he submitted to his sentence.
No; it is only God who can have given it to him.
So I greatly hope he has received the recompense
for it. The hearts of honest men willingly render
him the homage he deserves. Even the people, the
people who cried loudly for his death, said the next
day, and, indeed, on returning from the execution, ' But he protested his innocence on the gal-
lows: it was very wrong then not to have taken
him down.' "

The execution of M. de Favras afflicted Marie Antoinette not less than Madame Elisabeth: her chagrin
was even more keen because she was obliged to conceal it. On the Sunday following M. de la Villeurnoy
went in the morning to Madame Campan to say that

he intended to bring the widow and the son of the
Marquis de Favras to the public dinner of the King
and Queen. Madame Campan tried in vain to prevent this step. Madame de Favras and her son made
their appearance in deep mourning when dinner was
half over. But the Queen, behind whom was the
demagogue Santerre, commander of a battalion of
the National Guard, dared not say a single word to
the widow and the orphan. When the repast was
finished, she went to Madame Campan's room, and
throwing herself into an armchair, cried, "I am
come to weep with you." Then she added: "We
must needs perish when we are attacked by men who
unite every talent to every crime, and defended by
men who are very estimable, but have no adequate
idea of our position. They have compromised me
with both parties by presenting the wife and son of
Favras. If I were free to, I ought to have taken the
son of a man who had just sacrificed himself for us,
and placed him at table between the King and me;
but, surrounded by the executioners who had just
put his father to death, I did not even dare to look
at him. The royalists will blame me for seeming not
to have noticed the poor child, and the revolutionists
will be enraged at the thought that in presenting him
they expected to please me."

However, the Queen added that she understood
Madame de Favras's position, that she knew her to
be in need, and ordered Madame Campan to send
her next day several rolls of fifty louis each, assuring

her at the same time that the King and Queen would always provide for her and her son.

Poor Queen! What torture for a woman of her character! To be obliged to incessant dissimulation, to control her countenance, to hide her tears, to stifle her sighs, afraid to make known her sympathy and gratitude to her friends and advocates! Surrounded even in her palace by inquisitors, she dared neither to act nor speak. She hardly dared to think. What torture for a haughty and candid soul, for a woman who, notwithstanding, carried her head so high, for the daughter of the German Cæsars, for the Queen of France and Navarre!

V.

THE DAUPHIN AND MADAME ROYALE.

A WOMAN of the people, feeble, worn out with fatigue and poverty, sometimes reaches such an extreme of suffering and discouragement that she no longer feels the strength necessary to struggle against pain and hunger. But at the moment when she despairs, the poor woman casts a glance at her little children. Then her exhausted forces revive as by a miracle; the down-hearted creature rises up again. She will go on living; she will continue her fierce struggle against fate. Maternal tenderness converts her into a heroine.

Marie Antoinette suffered from neither poverty nor hunger. But her anguish was not on that account less keen. There are cruel anxieties beneath the gilded roofs of palaces as under the thatch of cabins, and when the Queen of France and Navarre felt her strength failing in her struggle up-stream, she had as much need to think of her children as the humble woman of the people. She was made intrepid by her passionate desire to save them. She suffered for them more than for herself. Anxiety about their future plunged her, as it were, into an abyss. Would the diadem that had been placed on the Dauphin's forehead prove a royal crown or a crown of thorns? Would the child to whom such a brilliant destiny had been promised be a king or a martyr? The maternal devotion of Marie Antoinette was both her joy and her affliction. The more unhappy she became, the more attached she was to the two children, at once her torment and her hope.

The once frivolous woman had become serious and grave. Far removed from her were all considerations of dress and elegance. No more distractions, no more theatres, no more balls, no more concerts, no more worldly conversations. Meditations only, prayers, long hours of needlework pursued with feverish activity, alms, good works, charitable excursions throughout Paris. The Queen of France had become the model of a Christian mother, the governess and teacher of her daughter. Her face, like her existence, had assumed something like austerity. The majesty which dominated her whole person was the supreme majesty of sorrow. Melancholy covered her as with a veil. Her days were passed in work, her nights were sleepless and unquiet. Her eyes, so often reddened by tears, were both tender and touching. She wrote to the Duchess de Polignac: "You speak of my courage. Less is needed to endure the frightful moments which present themselves than to bear up daily under our position with its peculiar pains, those of its friends, and of all those who surround us. It

is a load too heavy to be borne, and if my heart were
not so strongly bound to my husband, my children,
and my friends, I should desire to break down under
it. You all support me; I still owe this sentiment
to your friendship. For me, I bring misfortune to
every one, and your pains are for me and by me."

The queen might have weakened, but the mother
had not a moment of exhaustion. The sight of her
children gave her a courage equal to every trial. In
1790 her daughter, Madame Royale, was eleven
years old. The birth of this child had nearly cost
the mother's life. Madame Campan has described
the overflowing joy, the transports of delight, which
greeted the news that all danger was past. Madame
Campan deplores that a celestial voice, revealing the
secret decree of destiny, had not then cried to the
Queen's faithful servants: "Do not bless that art of
human beings which brings her back to life; weep,
rather, over her return to a world that is fatal and
cruel to the object of her affections. Ah! let her
quit it, honored, cherished. You will shed bitter
tears above her tomb; you can cover it with flowers.
. . . There will come a day when all the furies of
the earth, after having pierced her heart with a
thousand empoisoned shafts, after having graven the
signs of premature decrepitude on her noble and
touching features, will deliver her to tortures such
as do not exist for criminals; will deprive her
dead body of burial, and precipitate you all into the
same gulf with her if you permit the least movement

of compassion at the sight of so many cruelties to escape you."

Already disasters were hovering over the Queen's head. When Madame Royale came into the world, it was not a daughter but a son that the court desired. Marie Antoinette had only pressed the child more tenderly to her heart on that account. "Poor little one," she said to her, "you were not wanted, but for all that you will not be less dear to me. A son would have belonged more especially to the State. You will be my own, you will receive all my cares, you will share my happiness and sweeten my pains." Alas! there was no more happiness to share, but how many pains there were to sweeten!

Madame Royale displayed the best disposition, and from her infancy manifested those sentiments of piety which were the honor and consolation of her whole life. She made her first communion at the church of Saint Germain-l'Auxerrois on April 8, 1790. In the morning, Marie Antoinette led the young Princess into the King's chamber and said to her, "My daughter, throw yourself at your father's feet and ask his blessing." The child prostrated herself, and her father, raising her, addressed her in these words: "From the bottom of my heart I bless you, my daughter, asking Heaven to give you grace to appreciate well the great action you are going to perform. Your heart is innocent in the sight of God; your prayers should be pleasing to Him: offer them for your mother and me; ask Him to grant me the

grace necessary to secure the welfare of those whom
He has placed under my dominion and whom I ought
to consider as my children; ask Him to preserve the
purity of religion throughout the kingdom; and
remember well, my daughter, that this holy religion
is the source of happiness, and our pathway through
the adversities of life. Do not believe that you will
be sheltered from them; you are very young, but you
have already seen your father afflicted more than
once. You know not, my daughter, what Providence
has decreed for you, whether you will remain in this
realm or go away to live in another. In whatever
spot the hand of God may place you, remember that
you ought to edify by your example and to do good
whenever you find an opportunity. But above all,
my child, succor the unfortunate with all your might.
God gave us our birth in the rank we occupy only
that we might labor for their welfare and console
them in their afflictions. Go to the altar where you
are awaited, and implore the God of mercy never to
let you forget the counsels of a tender father." The
young Princess, profoundly moved, answered by her
tears.

It was customary for the daughters of France to
receive a set of diamonds on the day of their first
communion. Louis XVI. told Madame Royale that
he had done away with this too expensive usage.
"My daughter," he said, "I know your good sense
too well to permit me to suppose that at a moment
when you should be entirely occupied in preparing

your heart to be a sanctuary worthy of the Divinity, you can attach much value to artificial ornaments. Moreover, my child, public wretchedness is extreme, the poor abound everywhere, and assuredly you would rather go without jewels than know that they are going without bread."

The young Princess then went to her parish church, Saint Germain-l'Auxerrois. She approached the holy table with marks of the sincerest devotion. Marie Antoinette, in disguise, was present at the ceremony, which was of extreme simplicity and which produced in the royal family very sweet emotions. Louis XVI. gave abundant alms on this occasion. The day before, the Dauphin had said to his governess, Madame de Tourzel, "I am very sorry not to have my Versailles garden any more. I would have made two beautiful bouquets for to-morrow, one for my mother, and the other for my sister."

The Dauphin had just passed his fifth birthday (he was born March 27, 1785). The grace, the charming ways of the royal child fascinated even the demagogues. The Revolution grew milder when it saw him smile. The crowd never beheld him without emotion. He was so pretty, so cheerful, so amiable. He had been given, within the precinct of the Tuileries, at the end of the terrace beside the water, a little garden extending to the pavilion in-habited by his preceptor, the Abbé d'Avaux. There he found again what he had left behind him at Ver-

sailles, — air, amusement, flowers. When he went
to his new garden he was usually accompanied by
a detachment of the National Guard on duty at the
Palace of the Tuileries. He very often wore the
uniform of a National Guard. He learned the man-
ual exercise with a miniature gun, and nothing interested the crowd so much as to see him do the
exercise. When the spectators were not too numerous, he invited them to enter his garden.

One day when the throng was greater than usual,
and many persons seemed displeased not to be able
to come in, "Excuse me," said he, "I am very sorry
that my garden is so small, because that deprives me
of the pleasure of receiving all of you." Then he
offered flowers to those who approached the paling,
and looked pleasantly at them. A priest of the
parish of Saint Eustache, the Abbé Antheaume, conceived the idea of forming a regiment of children for
the little Prince: it was called the Royal Dauphin.
The uniform was a diminutive of that of the French
Guards, with white gaiters and a three-cornered hat.
This regiment of little boys asked to be treated in a
military manner, like the National Guard.

"There are no more children," said Lafayette.
"Very well, so be it! We have seen so many old
men possessing the vices of young ones that it is
good to see children display the virtues of men."
The infantine regiment served three posts of honor,
— the château of the Tuileries, the hotel of the
Mayor of Paris in the rue des Capucines, and that of

the commandant of the National Guard in the rue de Bourbon. When they marched past the royal family, Louis XVI. saluted the flag affectionately, and the Dauphin made gestures of sympathy to his little companions-in-arms.

Like the mother of the Gracchi, Marie Antoinette could say thereafter that her children were her jewels. The mother was still more august than the queen. Holding her son by one hand and her daughter by the other, she had an aspect at once imposing and sweet which ought to have disarmed the most ferocious hatred. But the Revolution was without pity and without bowels of compassion. Neither motherhood nor infancy could succeed in touching it.

VI.

THE ROYAL FAMILY AT SAINT CLOUD.

ONE experiences a singular sensation when, on leaving a city torn by civil war or revolution, he suddenly finds himself amidst the solitude and tranquillity of the country. In the presence of nature, so unmoved by our passions, man seems so little, God so great. It is a reconciliation, a truce, an oblivion. One almost persuades himself that he has nothing more in common with the city where he has suffered so much. A calm and gentle revery succeeds to cruel anxieties; one feels strengthened, consoled, rejuvenated.

This impression which Danton was afterwards to experience in the fields near Arcis-sur-Aube, Marie Antoinette enjoyed under the beautiful umbrage of Saint Cloud in the spring of 1790. The royal family, which was not yet absolutely captive, remained there from May 24 to the end of October. It was a great relief to hear revolutionary clamor no longer; to be out of the way of the vociferous hawkers who, at the Tuileries, were not contented to remain at the garden gates, but crossed it in every direction, announcing their threatening news. The Count and Countess of Provence did not live in the château of Saint Cloud, but they rented a house near the bridge and came every day to sup with the King and spend the evening.

Entire harmony reigned between all the members of the royal family. The rigid etiquette of former days was modified. The rule which permitted the admission of none but princes of the blood to the sovereign's table was relaxed. At dinner and supper the King and Queen invited persons to sit down with them nearly every day. After dinner they drove about the environs in open carriages. After supper the King played billiards with his family and his invited guests. He said one day to Mademoiselle Pauline de Tourzel, the daughter of his children's governess: —

"Pauline, can you play billiards?"

"No, Sire."

"Oh, well," went on Louis XVI., "you must know how to play billiards. I will take charge of your education and give you some lessons."

The good-natured King kept his word.

The stay at Saint Cloud was a lull in the storm. We who know the denouement of the drama in advance see nothing in its changing scenes but gloom and blood. The thought of the final catastrophe weighs upon us. The scaffold is always before our eyes. It haunts us incessantly. Happily, the reality was not always quite so frightful. A memory of

Charles I. rose up, it is true, in the obscurity; but, to
reassure themselves, people were wont to say that in
history similar situations rarely have identical con-
clusions. There were hours of calm, of hope, and
even of gaiety. The Countess de Béarn (Pauline
de Tourzel), in her *Souvenirs of Forty Years*, has
sketched the picture of this family life with its com-
parative tranquillity and its innocent distractions.
The Countess of Provence animated the conversations by her slightly malicious wit. She was
especially amusing on Sundays. On that day the
public were permitted to enter and walk around the
royal table. It was then the humor of the Princess
to guess at the character, disposition, and profession
of those who were passing before her. The sort of
prophetical examination which she made of their
faces sometimes led to very amusing results.

Madame Elisabeth enjoyed the stay at Saint Cloud.
"I have a window which opens on a tiny private
garden," she wrote to the Marquise de Bombelles;
"it gives me great pleasure. It is not so charming as
Montreuil, but at least I am free and can enjoy good
fresh air, which helps one to forget somewhat what is
going on — and you will agree that there is frequent
need of doing so." The little Dauphin had a fine
time at Saint Cloud. He was continually in the
garden, and went to walk every evening in the
park of Meudon.

Louis XVI., always inclined to optimism, like all
honest and kindly natures, felt his hopes revive, and

naïvely imagined that by dint of reading and meditating on the history of Charles I., he could find means to preserve himself from the fate of that unhappy monarch.

Alone among the royal family, Marie Antoinette had continual presentiments from which she could no more escape at Saint Cloud than at the Tuileries. Every contemporary memoir bears witness to the fixed idea which had pursued her since the outbreak of the Revolution, and the sort of vertigo caused her by the half-open abyss beneath her feet. Even at times when something like calm and forgetfulness stole over her mind, she remained profoundly sad; her whole person seemed enveloped in a veil of melancholy. She drew painful comparisons between the Saint Cloud of 1790 and the Saint Cloud of former years. The palace, the garden, the horizon, were the same, but how the light of other days was darkened! Where were now the times when the public thronged the park on Sunday evenings, and displayed such joy when the Queen with her children passed by in an open carriage, greeted by cheers and universal benedictions? Then, as Weber says, Saint Cloud offered the appearance of a great family reunion. No manner of uneasiness kept away the curious. The apartments, the gardens, the hearts of the august hosts, were open to the French people. Whither had vanished the epoch of the royal eclogue, when the amiable Queen patronized the rural ball? On the feast of Saint Cloud the peasants came in their best

attire, and the Queen gave them proofs of her gener-
osity, and sometimes joined in the dance like a simple
peasant. Where was the companionship of the Poli-
gnacs, so amusing, so brilliant, witty, and well pleased
with life? How swiftly those days of light-hearted
gaiety had fled away! Marie Antoinette, recalling
them, wrote from Saint Cloud to the self-exiled
Duchess de Polignac, "Ah, how sad is that dining-
room, once so gay!" On the horizon the fair city of
Paris, of old so beloved, so desired, how changed it
seems! Then it was the city of distractions, pleasures, and popular ovations, of gala representations,
ceremonious entries, visits to the Hôtel de Ville, of
Te Deums at Notre Dame, with salvos of applause
and murmurs of admiration when the Queen appeared — the Queen, that privileged being, almost
supernatural, more than woman, more than sovereign,
a sort of goddess, whose smile seemed like a celestial
benediction to the idolizing crowd. Paris is now
the hellish furnace of the Revolution, whose hot
breath penetrates even to the gardens of Saint Cloud,
to wither up the herbage, burn the greenery, and
corrupt the atmosphere. No, no; Paris was no longer
the good city, but the wicked city, the ungrateful,
arrogant, and cruel city, the city of spies, calumniators, persecutors, and, in a future, alas! very near,
the city of regicides.

At Paris, in the whirlpool of affairs, in the midst
of the mêlée, Marie Antoinette, as if the prey of an
evil dream, had not fully realized her situation. At

Saint Cloud she reflected more, she had leisure to feel herself live. It was then she reflected on the past, looked the present in the face, and questioned the future. She passed in review the different periods of her destiny, already so fertile in contrasts. She recalled the souvenirs of the Burg and of Schoenbrunn, of the chateau of Versailles, and the Little Trianon. One day she was walking in the park of Saint Cloud with Madame de Tourzel, the Duchess of Fitz-James, and the Princess of Tarente. Seeing herself surrounded by National Guards, some of whom were deserters from the French Guards, she said with tears in her eyes: " How surprised my mother would be if she could see her daughter, the child, the wife, and the mother of kings, or, at least, of an infant destined to become one, surrounded by a guard like this! It seems as if my father's mind was prophetic the day when I saw him for the last time."

Then she related to the three ladies who accompanied her that the Emperor Francis I., departing for Italy, whence he was never to return, had assembled his children about him to bid him farewell. " I was younger than my sisters," added Marie Antoinette; "my father took me on his knees, embraced me several times, and always with tears in his eyes, as if he felt great pain in leaving me. This appeared singular to all who were present; as for me, perhaps I should not have thought of it so often if my actual position, by recalling this circumstance, did not cause

me to dread for the remainder of my life a succession of misfortunes which it is only too easy to fore-
see." The impression which the Queen's last words
produced was so vivid that all three of the ladies
melted into tears. Then she said to them, with her
accustomed grace and sweetness: "I reproach myself
for having saddened you. Calm yourselves before
returning to the chateau. Let us revive our courage.
Providence will perhaps make us less unhappy than
we fear."

Saint Cloud was like an oasis in a desert parched
by the sun. It was a halt, a resting-place upon the
road to Calvary. In spite of her anxieties the Queen
enjoyed this last respite, this latest favor of fortune.
One might call it her farewell to the flowers, the
country, the nature she so much loved. Her dreamy
and poetic soul tasted with a sort of sad pleasure
those supreme joys which were to be torn away from
her so soon. She had still her husband, her children,
and her sister-in-law, that saintly Madame Elisabeth,
who watched beside royalty like a good angel. Ah!
while there is yet time, let us look well at this tranquil and patriarchal residence of Saint Cloud; at
these ancient trees which overshadow foreheads so
pure; at this noble royal family which, made sacred
by misfortune and fortified by religion, gives an
example of Christian virtues. It is an edifying spectacle, and consoles us; we are not willing to turn
away our eyes. Let us banish dismal images. They
will return but too quickly to dominate our thoughts.

VII.

THE only time that Marie Antoinette ever spoke with Mirabeau was at Saint Cloud, in private, on July 3, 1790, — a memorable interview, when two powerful influences came into each other's presence; that of genius and eloquence, and that of royalty and beauty, — an affecting interview which left the great tribune, as it were, fascinated, and which, had he lived longer, might have resulted in the salvation of the French monarchy. The most illustrious of orators and the most august and charming of queens found themselves face to face for one day only, and on that day they treated with each other as equal powers. But it was the woman who prevailed; it was her influence which carried off the honors of victory. The foeman of yesterday was the liegeman of to-morrow.

The man who succeeded in establishing relations between the court and Mirabeau was a great Belgian lord in the service of France, — Count de la Marck, younger son of the Duke of Arenberg. The correspondence between Mirabeau and Count de la Marck, collected, arranged, and annotated by M. de Bacourt, — a publication exceedingly interesting and of the greatest historical value, — gives details as curious as they are circumstantial concerning the part played by the famous tribune from the time when he became the secret agent of Louis XVI. while continuing to display the passions and speak the language of the Revolution.

Count de la Marck and Mirabeau became acquainted in 1788, and at once conceived a mutual sympathy. Mirabeau's genius attracted Count de la Marck, who, in his turn, charmed and fascinated Mirabeau by his courtesy, his good breeding, and his high social position. At bottom the great tribune was aristocratic. As the Duke of Levis has remarked in his *Souvenirs et Portraits*, "he loved the monarchy through reason, and the nobility through vanity, even to the point of putting his servants in livery so soon as his means permitted, and that in a period when other people were taking theirs out of it. He said one day to some Republican deputies, 'France will always need an aristocracy.'"

He was keenly chagrined by the fact that he was not thought well of in good society. Although by his birth he was on an equality with those who frequented the court, it was at once evident from his manners that he lacked the ease acquired by familiarity with the upper circles. He bowed too low when he wished to show politeness. He dressed in bad taste. Magnificent in the tribune, he was somewhat embarrassed on entering a drawing-room. He came in with an air of constrained gratitude which did not disappear until he was deep in conversation. "But then," says the Duke of Levis, "he quickly recovered his own place, which was the first."

The memory of his faults and of his adventurous life oppressed him. "Ah!" said he, "what injury the immorality of my youth has done to the public good!" He was the fifth child, but, by the death of a brother he became the eldest son of the Marquis of Mirabeau, a rich proprietor and the head of a great Provençal family. Married very young to a rich heiress, he served at first in the army, but presently abandoned both his wife and profession. At odds with his father, overwhelmed with debts, reduced to expedients, thrown into prison by arbitrary orders under the King's privy seal, obliged to live on his scanty earnings as an author, going from one irregularity to another, and from scandal to scandal, he got the reputation of a degraded and unworthy person. He threw himself into the revolutionary camp through bitterness and vexation.

But this rôle did not fail to shock his secret instincts. He prided himself on his good birth, and suffered because he could not live in accordance with his hereditary rank. When, after the suppression of titles and coats-of-arms he found himself designated in the reports of the sessions of the National Assembly under the plebeian appellation, Riquetti Senior, called Mirabeau, his old feudal pride revolted in the tribune's soul. In the depth of his heart he cursed the arrogant Revolution which dared deprive him of his title as Count. He was enraged with himself for having served it, and muttered by way of excuse that he meant to war against it and hoped to be its master. The seeming demagogue was in reality a remorseful monarchist. Count de la Marck says: " On several occasions when I was irritated by his revolutionary language in the tribune, I flew into a violent passion and berated him soundly. Well! he would burst into tears like a child, and without baseness express his contrition with a sincerity which no one could doubt."

Such was the man whom M. de la Marck found means to reconcile with the court. At first the task was not easy. The Queen's prejudices against the tribune seemed at first glance invincible. Toward the close of 1789 she wrote to M. de la Marck: "I have never doubted your sentiments, and when I learned that you were in league with Mirabeau I thought, assuredly, that it was with the best intentions. But you can accomplish nothing with him; and as to what you consider necessary on the part of the King's ministers, I do not agree with you. We shall never, I think, be so unfortunate as to be reduced to the painful necessity of having recourse to Mirabeau."

A few weeks later things had changed. In March, 1790, Count de la Marck, who was in Belgium, was recalled to Paris by a word from Count de Mercy-

Argenteau, the Austrian Ambassador, and a friend of
Marie Antoinette. The Queen had at last decided
to take counsel with Mirabeau, and it was Count de
la Marck whom she charged with the negotiation in
the name of the King. Count de la Marck made
known the conditions to his friend.

Mirabeau was to receive six thousand livres a
month, and all his debts, to the amount of two hundred and eight thousand livres, would be paid. It
was, moreover, the King's intention to send him a
million, if, at the close of the session of the National
Assembly, he had fulfilled his engagements with the
court faithfully. Never had Mirabeau been more
rejoiced than by this news. Proud because his King
had recourse to him, happy to pass in the twinkling
of an eye from straitened circumstances to fortune,
enraptured, enthusiastic, full of gratitude, he was in
a sort of intoxication.

The thing is done. The revolutionist becomes
conservative. In appearance he will be still a tribune. But at bottom he is a monarchist, a defender
and servant of Louis XVI., a secret agent of the
court, who sends note after note and gives counsel
upon counsel. He wrote thus, May 10, 1790, in his
first letter to the sovereign: " Profoundly moved by
the anguish of the King, who has least merited his
personal misfortunes, persuaded that if in his situation there is a prince whose word may be relied on,
that prince is Louis XVI., I am, nevertheless, so
armed by men and events against the compassion

which springs from the sight of human vicissitudes,
that I should experience an invincible repugnance
against playing a part in this moment of factions and
confusion, if I were not convinced that the re-establishment of the King's legitimate authority is the
prime necessity of France, and the only means of saving it. But I see clearly that we are in anarchy and
are sinking more deeply in it daily; I am so indignant at the idea that I shall have contributed merely
to a vast demolition, and the fear of seeing any one
but the King at the head of the state is so insupportable to me, that I feel imperiously summoned back to
public affairs at the moment when, vowed in a certain
sense to the silence of contempt, I thought only of
aspiring to retirement."

And in the same letter he promises to the sovereign "loyalty, zeal, activity, energy, and a courage of
which no one, perhaps, has any just idea." He promises "all, in fact, except success, which never depends
on one alone." Some days afterwards he wrote, in
the ardor of his royalistic zeal: "I have professed
monarchical principles when I saw nothing in the
court but its feebleness, and when, knowing neither
the soul nor the thoughts of the daughter of Maria
Theresa, I could not count on that august auxiliary.
I have fought for the rights of the throne when I
inspired nothing but distrust, and when every act of
mine, envenomed by malignity, seemed like a snare.
I have served the monarch when I knew very well
that I need expect neither rewards nor benefits from a

just but deluded king. What will I not do now, when confidence has increased my courage, and when recognition has converted my principles into my duties?"

Mirabeau had not yet had the honor of speaking with Marie Antoinette, but he was already her enthusiastic admirer. June 20, 1790, he wrote in one of his notes for the court: "The King has only one man; it is his wife. There is no safety for her but in the re-establishment of the royal authority. I should like to believe that she would not desire life without her crown; but what I am very certain of is, that she will not preserve her life if she does not preserve her crown. The time will come, and very soon, when she will have to try what a woman and child can do on horseback — for her that is a family fashion; but, meanwhile, it is necessary to make preparations, and not believe it possible, whether by the aid of chance or of combinations, to escape from an extraordinary crisis by the assistance of ordinary men and measures."

The providential, the extraordinary man will be himself, the Count de Mirabeau. He who has converted the tribune into the gigantic pedestal of his renown, his pride; he who, his heart fascinated by his own genius, his ears filled with the echoes of his thunderous voice, takes pleasure in the magnificent expansion of his triumphant personality, do you know what he aspires to as the greatest of his victories? A word, a smile, from Marie Antoinette. His chief desire is to present his homage to the Queen.

On July 3, 1790, this desire was at last realized. It was agreed that the interview should take place secretly at Saint Cloud. To conceal the proceeding, Mirabeau did not spend the previous night at Paris, but at Auteuil, at the house of his niece, Madame d'Aragon. He was afterwards conducted with great mystery to the designated place of the political rendezvous. This, according to Madame Campan's account, was not an apartment of the palace, as M. de Lacretelle relates, but at the meeting of the paths in the high grounds of the Queen's private garden at Saint Cloud.

Behold, then, the tribune and the sovereign face to face. Consider that interview wherein the royalty of birth and the royalty of genius experience a reciprocal shudder as they contemplate each other. He is there, then, the man whom for more than a year the Queen has thought of as an object of terror, a sort of antichrist, whom she has called the monster. It is hardly nine months since he was described to her as a savage being, directing bands of brigands coming from Paris to Versailles to slay her. It was a calumny, but she had believed it. She recalled the body-guards assassinated while defending her; her palace, her bedchamber, invaded by cannibals who demanded her head. She heard incessantly the sinister echo of furious cries, the cries of death; and to all these souvenirs the menacing image of Mirabeau clung like a phantom. And now he was before her, that man of terrific ugliness, whose eyes flashed light-

ning; massive, and tall in stature; his strong head
large beyond all ordinary measure, and still further
amplified by an enormous mass of hair which resembled a lion's mane.

Behold him, this Titan of speech, this Atlas who
would bear up a world! And who, then, will be
most intimidated by this meeting, the Queen or the
tribune? It is he, he especially who is moved, he
who has a shock of admiration and respect. Formidable orator, you who in the tribune seem able to
knead marble with your gigantic hands; you whose
supernatural voice is like the trump of the last judgment; you who, at your own will unchain or calm
the tempests; at your feet all the fury of the multi-
tudes would feebly expire — and yet the rustle of a
woman's dress and the sound of her voice make you
tremble!

Gentle, benevolent, august, the Queen addresses
the tribune with the supreme grace of which she has
the secret: "With an ordinary foe," she said to him,
"with a man who might have sworn the downfall of
monarchy without appreciating its utility to a great
people, I should be at this moment taking a most im-
proper step; but when one speaks to a Mirabeau. . . ."

Marie Antoinette went on in her most affable tone,
and each of her words penetrated to the very depths
of Mirabeau's soul. Ah! how much more the presence of this Queen, so fair, so noble, and so unhappy,
flatters the French Demosthenes than all the triumphs
of the tribune, all the intoxication of popularity!

How he ranks the least word from that sacred mouth
above the most enthusiastic acclamations, the most
frenzied applause of the National Assembly. Oh!
he, at least, does not deceive himself like Cardinal
de Rohan. It is not a false Queen there in the shrub-
bery this time. It is the real Marie Antoinette, the
daughter of the German Cæsar, the child of Maria
Theresa, the wife of the descendant of Henri IV.
and Louis XIV., the Queen of France and Navarre!
What an honor, what a rehabilitation, to be well
received by such a woman! Mirabeau is contented
with himself. He feels proud and happy. All
his remorse vanishes. All that has been evil in
his past is but a dream. He opens a new career;
he no longer doubts the future. Full of hope and
full of faith, it is with profound conviction that he
cries, in taking leave of the Queen, "Madame, the
monarchy is saved!"

VIII.

IN July, 1790, the royal family left Saint Cloud for several days and went to Paris to be present at the fêtes of the Federation. Never had the populace been so preoccupied with any solemnity. The *Moniteur* described it as an "august fête, the most majestic and imposing which, since the annals of the world have been known to us, has honored the human race." The men of the French Revolution delighted in everything theatrical. Mythological pomps, souvenirs of antiquity, grandiose spectacles, enraptured them, and nothing so charmed the Parisians as open-air ceremonies in which they were both actors and spectators.

The day chosen for the fête was July 14, the anniversary of the taking of the Bastille. The King, the members of the National Assembly, the army, and delegates from every department of France, were to assemble on the Champ-de-Mars and take a solemn oath to support the new Constitution. The people naïvely imagined that this Constitution was going to be the source of order, peace, liberty, progress, pros-

perity, and a state of things which would bring back
to earth the age of gold. The Hebrews in the
desert had not awaited with more impatience the
Holy Law which Moses brought down to them from
Sinai. And yet, as nearly always happened at the
time of the Revolution, a secret disquiet mingled
with these illimitable hopes and joys.

A few days before the fête, the Duke of Orleans,
coming from England, where he had sojourned since
the October days in a sort of exile, disguised under
the title of a diplomatic mission, arrived in Paris, and
in the evening made his appearance at the palace.
This unexpected arrival alarmed everybody. It was
believed that the Duke, badly received by the King,
and almost insulted by the court, was about to
organize a great conspiracy. The people, always
credulous, believed the most contradictory and fabu-
lous reports. Conservatives and revolutionists alike
lent themselves to the most terrifying projects. According to some, an insurrection was about to break
out in Paris; the deputies of the nobility would be
massacred on the Champ-de-Mars; Louis XVI. would
be deprived of his crown, and the Duke of Orleans
placed on the throne. According to others, there was
to be a counter-revolution; the patriots would have
their throats cut, and the most popular members of
the National Assembly would be shot; the suburbs
would be burned, and Louis XVI., leaving the Champ-
de-Mars, would re-enter the Tuileries as an absolute
monarch. This panic did not last long. The multi-

tude, always fickle, soon lost all fear, and busying
themselves in preparations for the fête with a passionate activity which bordered on frenzy, they became absorbed in sentiments of confidence and joy.

Twelve thousand workmen were constantly employed in the Champ-de-Mars, where, by means of
circular terraces, they were about to form a gigantic
amphitheatre, whose benches would seat three hundred thousand spectators. It was an immense piece
of work. As it was feared that they might not be
able to finish it by July 14, and as this revolutionary
date was deemed essential, the districts, in the name
of the country, invited all good citizens to come to
the aid of the workmen in the Champ-de-Mars with
shovels and wheelbarrows. This invitation, so con-
formable to the patriotic ideas of the time, excited
general enthusiasm. Through fashion and infatua-
tion, still more than through patriotism, everybody
saw in this labor both a pleasure and a duty.

According to Camille Desmoulins, the day which
is approaching is " the day of deliverance from Egyptian bondage, and the crossing of the Red Sea; it is
the first day of the year One of Liberty ; it is the
day predicted by the prophet Ezekiel, — the day of
destiny, the great feast of the lanterns." Patriots of
all classes, men and women, old men and children,
rich and poor — which of you is unwilling to aid in
making ready the splendors of such a solemnity?
Come then, one and all, to join this immense band of
laborers where, as the Marquis de Ferrières has said,

"the dishevelled courtesan finds herself next to a shamefaced virgin; where the Capuchin hauls a dray with the chevalier of Saint Louis, the porter with the coxcomb from the Palais Royal; where the robust herring-woman pushes the wheelbarrow loaded by the fashionable and hypochondriacal lady."

"It is the ballet of the reunion of classes," says Camille Desmoulins. It is like a great Flemish festival. People sing while they work. The perambulating eating-houses, the portable shops, add to the animation of the scene. Do you hear the buffooneries, the songs, the noise of drums and trumpets, the spades, the wheelbarrows, the voices of the laborers who call to and encourage each other? Do you see these Seminarists, these Carthusians, who have left their cloisters to come to this civic rendezvous? Do you see these marquises who take off their gloves to shake hands with charcoal-dealers? They say that Saint Just, pushing a wheelbarrow, met the Countess du Barry, with a shovel in her hand. A disabled soldier of Louis XIV.'s day is working with his wooden leg. What activity reigns amid these hundred and fifty thousand voluntary laborers! So much zeal ends by accomplishing the desired result. The terraces are finished. The Champ-de-Mars is ready. How the patriots rejoice! Behold the Fourteenth of July, the great day!

The Federates, ranged by departments, under eighty-three banners, have been assembled since daybreak on the Place de la Bastille. Deputies, soldiers of the line, and marine troops, the Parisian National Guard, drummers, bands of singers, and the banners of the sections open and close the march. The immense procession passes through the streets of Saint Martin, Saint Denis, and Saint Honoré. On reaching the Tuileries, its ranks are swelled by the municipal officials and the Assembly. It passes on through the Cours la Reine and enters the Champ-de-Mars by a bridge of boats which has been constructed across the stream. At the end of this bridge rises a triumphal arch, on which may be read the following mottoes : —

"We fear you no longer, petty tyrants,
    You who oppressed us under a hundred different names."

"The rights of man have been disregarded for centuries; they have been re-established for all humanity."

"The king of a free people is the only powerful king."

Another motto may also be read, which will not be pondered sufficiently : —

"You cherish this liberty, you possess it now; show yourselves worthy to preserve it."

Three hundred thousand spectators are crowded together on the sides of the amphitheatre. They have been there since six in the morning. The weather is bad. The showers produce a singular effect. As soon as it begins to rain, thousands of different colored umbrellas are opened, and change

the aspect of the terraces. The Federates, dripping
with water and perspiration, are no longer gay and in
high spirits. To pass away the time, the first comers
begin a Provençal dance. Those who follow them
join in, and form a circle which soon embraces a large
portion of the Champ-de-Mars. Not contented with
dancing, the Federates engage in mock combats;
cities against country places, departments against departments, Provençaux against Flemings, Lorrainers
against Bretons. These little wars terminate in fra-
ternal embraces. Then the dances begin again, better than ever.

The delighted spectators beat time, and applaud.
The foreigners cry, "Look at these devils of Frenchmen who dance while it is raining fast." Who cares
for bad weather when the sun in the heart is shining?
Finally, the entire procession is about to enter the
Champ-de-Mars. The games cease, and every Federate returns to his own banner.

The circumference of the circus, on the side of the
buildings of the Military School, is closed by a large
covered gallery, ornamented with blue and gold
hangings, in the midst of which is a pavilion intended
for the King. Behind the throne is a private box for
the Queen, the Dauphin, and the Princesses of the
royal family. The sovereign being no longer more
than half a sovereign, until the time should come
when he would not be even that, there had been
placed beside his throne, and about three feet distant,
another armchair of the same size, covered with

azure velvet, sown with golden lilies: it was destined
for the President of the National Assembly. A vast
altar rose in the middle of the immense space encir-
cled by the amphitheatre. It was twenty-five feet
high. It was ascended by four staircases terminating
in a platform, where incense was burned in antique
vases. On the south front of this altar these two
distichs might be read : —

> " Mortals are equal ; it is not their birth,
> It is their virtue differences their worth."

> " Throughout the State, the Law should reign supreme,
> Equal, to her, are men, howe'er they seem."

On the opposite side angels were represented, sounding trumpets bearing these inscriptions : —

> " Consider these three sacred words: the Nation, the Law,
> the King. The Nation is You. The Law, again, is You. The
> King is the guardian of the Law."

On the side facing the Seine might be distinguished an image of Liberty, and a Genius hovering
in the air with a pennon on which was written,
" Constitution."

Three hundred priests, vested in white albs, and
wearing tricolored scarfs, cover the steps of the
altar. Talleyrand, Bishop of Autun, and a member
of the National Assembly, is about to say the Mass.
The office begins. Fortunately, the clouds disperse,
and the sun comes out. Chants, military music, and

salvos of artillery mingle with the bishop's voice. At
the Elevation the drums beat a salute; the trumpets
sound; the whole crowd are on their knees. The
Mass ended, Lafayette dismounts from his white
horse, and walks over to the galleries where the
King, the royal family, the Ministers, and the members of the National Assembly are seated, and ascend-
ing the fifty steps leading to the throne of Louis XVI.,
receives the commands of the sovereign, who hands
to him the formula of the appointed oath. Turning
afterwards toward the altar, Lafayette lays his sword
upon it, and, going up to its most elevated point, he
gives the signal for the oath by waving a flag in air.

The hundred pieces of artillery, the two thousand
brass instruments, the hundreds of thousands of
spectators, all are silent. In this religious silence
one voice alone is heard: the voice of Lafayette.
Laying one hand on his heart, and lifting the other
toward heaven, he pronounces these words: "We
swear to be always faithful to the nation, the law,
and the King; to maintain with all our power the
Constitution decreed by the National Assembly, and
accepted by the King; to protect, comformably with
the laws, the security of person and property, the
traffic in grains and other provisions in the interior
of the kingdom, the collection of public taxes under
whatever form they exist, and to remain united to
all Frenchmen by the indissoluble ties of fraternity."

Then all arms are flung up, all swords brandished,
and an immense cry breaks forth: "I swear it." The

artillery of neighboring municipalities announces the
oath to more distant ones, which, in their turn, trans-
mit it in like manner, and with lightning swiftness,
to the very extremities of France: to France transformed in an instant into an immense Champ-de-
Mars, where twenty-five millions of French Federates
swear, at the same moment, to defend the law, to be
faithful to the sovereign, and to live and die for
their country. Louis XVI. rises and pronounces
these words in a strong voice: "I, King of the
French, swear to employ the power delegated to me
by the constitutional act of the State, in maintaining
the Constitution decreed by the National Assembly,
and by me accepted." The Queen takes the Dauphin
in her arms, and, presenting him to the people,
"Behold my son," says she; "he joins, as I do, in
the same sentiments." From every breast break forth
these cries, repeated with wild enthusiasm: "Long
live the King! Long live the Queen! Long live
Monseigneur the Dauphin!" The weather is completely settled. No more clouds; the sun shines in
full splendor.

Who would not feel his hopes revive in presence
of this colossal demonstration, this delirium of good-
will and reconciliation? Optimism is in the air. It
is an irresistible current. How can one be severe on
the generous illusions of the unfortunate Louis XVI.,
remembering that these illusions were not his alone,
but those of a whole nation? At this hour the monarchy is regarded as the best of republics. People

and into ecstasies over the merits and virtues of the patriot-King. It is like a picture by Greuze which should suddenly become an incommensurable fresco. One might say that the old régime and the Revolution, reconciled once for all, are exchanging the kiss of peace, and pressing each other in a cordial embrace. Brethren uniting tenderly around an exemplary father of a family, — such was the tableau presented by the Champ-de-Mars. Woe to him, who, in this innumerable multitude, should venture a single word of doubt concerning the future! Woe to him who would have the temerity to disbelieve in the resurrection of the age of gold!

A *Te Deum* with full orchestra is about to terminate the ceremony. It is five o'clock in the afternoon. The Federates go in good order to the chateau of La Muette, where a grand banquet, served in the alleys of the park, is awaiting them. Out of bed from dawn to midnight, they have walked from their homes to the Place de la Bastille, from there to the Champ-de-Mars, from the Champ-de-Mars to La Muette, from La Muette back to their lodgings. They have danced, cried, sung, and been drenched with torrents of rain; and still they are enthusiastic, rapt to the seventh heaven. It must be admitted that this vigorous generation, which, some years later, was to perform so many brilliant deeds, so many prodigies on every battle-field of Europe, braves fatigue and danger with an ardor and animation which excuse many faults.

The rejoicings lasted for several days. At the Barrière de l'Étoile the King held a grand review. The Queen was present in an open carriage with the Dauphin and Madame Elisabeth. She spoke with exquisite politeness to all who approached her, and more than one Federate had the honor of kissing her hand. In the evening, the municipality gave a grand popular fête. The two principal points of reunion were on the Place de la Bastille and the Champs-Élysées. Where the former prison had stood there was a ball, and this inscription: "Dancing here." In the evening no carriages could pass. Everybody was obliged to go on foot. Everybody was happy to show that he belonged to the people.

The Champs-Élysées presented a fairy-like aspect, with its lights depending from every tree, its wreaths of lanterns, its pyramids of flame. "It was at the Champs-Élysées," said the Marquis de Ferrières, "that sensible men took most satisfaction in the fête. The citizen, with his family, ate, chatted, walked about, and was agreeably conscious of his existence. Young girls and boys were dancing to the music of bands placed here and there in open spaces among the trees. . . . A sweet and sentimental joy visible on all faces, and shining in every eye, recalled the placid enjoyment of happy shades in the Elysian fields of the ancients. The white garments of a multitude of women straying amid the trees of these fine avenues added to the illusion."

O dreams too swiftly vanished! Chimeras which

the terrible reality will presently cause to disappear!
Strange festivals where reconciliation lies on the sur-
face while hatred and passion live still within the
depths. Envy and rancor pierce through these idyls,
these gigantic eclogues. People sing the *Ça ira*: —

> " *Ça ira, ça ira,*
> To the lamp-posts with the aristocrats;
> *Ça ira, ça ira,*
> The aristocrats, we'll hang them all!"

A sagacious observer might readily have foreseen
that to the three words, Liberty, Equality, Fraternity, there would speedily be added this conclusion of the formula: "Or Death." The Mass was
preceded by a dance. No doubt the patriots reminded
each other that David danced before the ark. Why
should not they dance before the altar of the Federation? No matter! This mixture of patriotism and
religion makes a poor alloy. Such an ecclesiastic as
the Bishop of Autun seems hardly the man to
invoke the blessings of the Lord upon the crowds
assembled in the Champ-de-Mars. There is more
mythology than Christianity in the whole affair.

Optimists, do not rejoice! Yet a little while, and
these honest royalists, these tender-hearted people,
who come with the Federates of Béarn to shed tears
of filial tenderness at the foot of the statue of Henri
IV., will be howling with rage around the scaffold
of his descendant.

Who are the three men that come most noticeably
to the front in the fête of the Champ-de-Mars? A

king, a general, and a bishop. The king is the future martyr; the general, the future prisoner of Olmutz; the bishop is the future exile, the priest who throws away his chasuble, cross, and mitre. The Mass celebrated by this pontiff will not bring good fortune either to Louis XVI. or to France!

IX.

MIRABEAU'S interview with Marie Antoinette had made a profound impression on him. The royal vision remained in his eyes and in his heart as a kind of bewildering dream. He wept with remorse when he thought that formerly he might have been esteemed the enemy of this beautiful sovereign. He wept with joy in reminding himself that thenceforward he would be her knight, her defender. Certain suspicions concerning this sudden conversion of the famous tribune got into circulation. An article published in a daily paper, *L'Orateur du Peuple*, accused him of having gone to Saint Cloud, and insinuated that he must have seen the Queen. Mirabeau admitted that he had left Paris to pay a visit to his niece, Madame d'Aragon, but declared that the alleged interview at Saint Cloud was purely imaginary. Things rested there, although for several days accounts of the "Great treason of Count Mirabeau" were hawked about the streets of Paris.

To kindle and extinguish conflagrations, to unchain and quiet tempests, to be by turns revolutionists and

71

conservatives, destroyers and preservers, is the dream of ambitious men who imagine themselves able to play with human passions like an Indian juggler with his bowls, and who frequently believe themselves the masters of events when in reality they are merely their slaves. During several months it was possible for Mirabeau to play a double part without being unmasked; but had he lived longer, the deception could not have been kept up, and the great man, driven into a corner, would have been forced to make his choice between the two selves — the royalist and the tribune — that were incarnated in him.

All energetic men, no matter who they may be, have the governing instinct, and their aim, if they hope to arrive at power, is order and domination. Revolution is not an end, but a means to most great agitators, and there are few demagogues who do not long to be all-powerful. Mirabeau's ideal was to become the strong and influential minister of an undisputed king, crushing all resistance with his iron hand, and saying with an absolute voice to the revolutionary flood: "Thou shalt go no further."

A socialist journal, published at Verviers, calls itself *The Mirabeau.* This journal is doubtless not well acquainted with the part assumed by the great tribune during the last months of his life. I suspect that the democrats of our day would not feel disposed to approve the ideas and principles he professed. It is rather singular to recall how the great-

est orator of the French Revolution judged Paris,
the National Assembly, and the National Guard, if
not in the tribune, at least in the privacy of his conscience.

Desire for a reaction went to the length of Machi-
avellianism in the mind of the tribune, now become
the secret agent of the court. He wished to lay
snares for the Assembly, and make it the victim of
its own faults and outrages. He even became a disciple of that school which, in all epochs of disorder,
expresses the hope that good must be born from the
excess of evil. He had two policies, two faces. He
lived a double life, — the revolutionist on this side,
the royalist on that. The equilibrium he continued
to preserve between them was almost miraculous.
There was so much force, skill, and eloquence in this
powerful actor, that even his adversaries dared not
suspect him. His popularity was like a sturdy oak
which defies wind and lightning.

Nevertheless, this double part has something essen-
tially disagreeable about it. When one thinks of the
man who had just fulminated demagogic invectives
in the tribune, returning to his own house, and sitting
down in private to write his communications to the
court, it is impossible not to be distressed by a duplicity which would have needed to be unhired in
order to be excused. Assuredly Mirabeau pursued
a plan approved by his conscience. But, for all that,
he remains, in spite of all his genius and his glory, a
man who was obliged to skulk, who received hush-

money, who would have been ruined completely in public opinion if his writings and his actions had suddenly been made known. Like all talented men whose conscience troubles them, he was at once haughty and humble; haughty when he was on view before men, humble when he entered within himself. His Atlas shoulders, huge and powerful as they were, bent under the intolerable burden of his double part. He would have liked to be himself before God and men.

Let us interrogate the depths of his soul. Let us see him as he is. Let us ask his opinions of men and things. Parisians, this is what he has to say of your city, so well satisfied with itself: " Never were so many combustible elements and inflammable materials brought together on a single hearth. A hundred scribblers whose sole resource is disorder, a multitude of insubordinate strangers who kindle discord in all public places, . . . all that is most corrupt in both extremes, — the dregs of the nation and the most elevated classes, — and this is Paris. This city knows its strength. It has exercised it by turns on the army, the King, the Ministers, and the Assembly. It is certain that Paris is the last city in the kingdom to which peace will be restored. It is necessary, therefore, to destroy its influence in the provinces, to make its projects dreaded, to show the expenses of every sort which it occasions, and to make the people desire that a second legislative body shall be placed in a city where its independence and

the King's liberty will be more secure." (47th Note
to the Court, December 23, 1790.)

Partisans of the National Guard, listen to what
Mirabeau has to say in the same note of that insti-
tution: "I consider the National Guard of Paris as
an obstacle to the restoration of order. . . . This
troop is too numerous to have any *esprit de corps*,
too closely united to the citizens ever to resist them,
too easy to corrupt, not in masses, but as individuals,
not to be an instrument always ready to serve the
seditious."

You who respect the parliamentary system so
greatly, do you wish to know how Mirabeau thought
the National Assembly should be treated? In the
same note he writes: "I have already pointed out
several ways of attacking the Assembly. They may
be reduced chiefly to these: Let it issue every decree
which may increase the number of malcontents; in-
cite it to destroy the rural municipalities, to change
the organizations of those of cities, and to put a check
on the administration of departments; get up popular petitions to it on points known to be out of harmony with its principles; push it further toward
usurping all powers; make its discussions bear on
unimportant topics; have the minority introduce the
most popular motions, so that they may be thrown
out or modified; prolong the session until the abuses
of the new judiciary order, and the difficulty in the
way of imposing taxes, shall become thoroughly
known; acquaint it every day with the obstructions

which hinder the execution of its laws, and demand that it shall explain them itself; and, in fine, neglect at the same time no opportunity to augment the popularity of the Queen and the King. There is no room for hesitation; if this Assembly runs its course triumphantly, the state of public opinion permits no further hope."

The devoted agent of the court, Mirabeau thus insists on the importance of the advice he gives it:—

"Everything may be hoped if my plan is adopted; and if it is not, if this last plank of safety escapes us, there is no misfortune, from individual assassinations to pillage, from the downfall of the throne to the dissolution of the empire, which may not be anticipated. What other resource exists except this plan? Is not the ferocity of the people increasing by degrees? Are they not being induced to hope for the division of property? . . . Could frenzy and fanaticism be pushed to a higher point than they are in the National Assembly? Unhappy nation! Behold whither you have been led by men who have put intrigue in the place of talent! Honest but feeble King! unfortunate Queen! look down into the frightful abyss to which your fluctuations between a too blind confidence and an exaggerated distrust have conducted you! One effort can still be made by each of you; but it is the last. If it is not attempted, or if it fails, a funereal pall is about to envelop this empire. What will be its destiny? Whither will drift this vessel, struck by the lightning

and beaten by the storm? I do not know; but if I
make my own escape from the public wreck, I shall
always say with pride in my retirement, 'I exposed
myself to ruin in order to save them all, and they
would not.' "

We have just seen in Mirabeau the extreme conservative, the ardent reactionist, the man of order,
discipline, authority, the zealous, convinced, enthusiastic royalist. And yet in the tribune it still
often happened to him to display revolutionary sentiments. If there was talk of hoisting the tricolor
instead of the white flag upon the government vessels, or of the pillage of the Hôtel de Castries by
the people, or some other burning question, the demagogue, the agitator, reappeared at once. Intoxicated
by the applause which greeted his fiery harangues,
he became again the idol of the multitude, and delighted in his popularity. Like great actors who play
successively two different parts with equal talent and
conviction, he forgot perhaps, for a moment, that he
was a reactionist, an enemy of the National Assembly, a secret agent of the Tuileries. He was like
those consummate advocates, who feel they possess
sufficient address and eloquence to argue both their
own cause and the opposing one. There was room
in this exuberant and fiery nature for both the Revolution and the counter-revolution. He was the engine
and the brake, the torrent and the dike.

O powerful orator, amuse yourself with your
genius! May your eloquence give you, if not the

joys of a patriot, at least those of an artist! Win the
applause of this Assembly which hardly suspects that
you are the man who most opposes it! Listen to
yourself talk! May the majesty of your voice en-
chant your own ears! May the captivating influence
of your discourse carry you away from earth! All
this will not last much longer. Both you and the
monarchy are condemned to a speedy end. Your
popularity can accomplish nothing for the welfare of
France. You, who hardly desire anything but storms
and shipwrecks, strive vainly to-day to play the pilot.
The sea is too rough, the tempest too formidable, and
you can no more reason with the Revolution than
with the dead. Let the crew tremble, then! You
try in vain to save them. It is too late.

X.

THE DEPARTURE OF THE KING'S AUNTS.

A BREACH had opened in the ranks of the King's adherents. The most ardent supporters of the monarchy were no longer at hand to defend it. Through a mistaken notion of honor, the royalists gloried in abandoning their sovereign, the military in deserting the field of battle. The court ladies despised the young men who would not emigrate. The nobility departed as if for a rendezvous of patriotism and monarchical fidelity. Those who remained in France hardly dared to show themselves. Great ladies sent them distaffs, symbols of cowardice. People emigrated through vanity, or conceit, or because it was the fashion. It was said that the King's brothers knew better than any one what comported with his service, and that, if they had thought it right to betake themselves to foreign lands, the place of the faithful nobility was also there. It was added that all that would be necessary to crush the impertinent Revolution, was to show one's crest. "It will last about two weeks," said the earliest fugitives.

Louis XVI., always weak and fluctuating, had

neither the courage to approve nor to disavow the emigration. Officially, he condemned it, but at bottom he hoped to make it useful. He had in it not merely relatives, friends, and servants, but agents. It inspired him by turns with fear and sympathy. Sometimes he saw a danger in it, and again a last chance of safety. At one moment he criticised the emigrants, at another he would have been glad to be among them. The sovereign, perhaps, treated them as conspirators, but the man, the husband, and the father told himself that these conspirators might well become the saviours of his wife and children. Not knowing clearly what he wished, the unfortunate monarch was drawn in different directions. It happened to him, the best and most well-intentioned man in the kingdom, to play a double part, and to incarnate in himself two kings, — the king of the tricolor and the king of the white flag. Ah! woe to the epochs when the notion of right becomes obscured, when conscience, virtue, and patriotism, being interrogated, know not what to answer! Happy the people among whom one may serve his country regularly and without hesitation, where duty is precise, incontestable, and uncontested, where the same fact is not at the same time characterized as loyal and as criminal, as fidelity and as treason!

Even while disavowing the emigration, the court was in secret relations with it. That was what caused the uneasy suspicions which disquieted the multitude and made them cast anxious glances across

the frontiers. They had a presentiment that Louis
XVI. would flee from Paris, and the very people
who rendered the royal family so unhappy could not
become accustomed to the idea of seeing them go
away. This explains the extreme excitement felt
when the King's aunts left Bellevue to go to Rome.
No one cared much about these Princesses; they lived
in a sort of retirement and took no part in politics.
But it was feared lest their departure might prove
the signal for that of the King and Queen. Moreover, the resolution adopted by the ladies resulted in
recalling public attention to the emigration, that
burning question which was one of those that most
inflamed the imagination of the people.

Mesdames Adelaide and Victoire, daughters of Louis
XV., and aunts of Louis XVI., had essayed to make
themselves forgotten from the beginning of the Revolution. They lived in a retired manner at their chateau
of Bellevue, occupying themselves solely in works of
charity, but regretting the old régime and sharing all
the ideas of the emigrants. Like their father, they
had a horror of newfangled opinions, and whether
in religion or politics, were profoundly devoted to
retrograde principles. When the Revolution grew
more pronounced, it became insupportable to them to
remain in France. They had only one idea, — to
quit a country polluted by disorder, and go to Rome
to kneel in the basilica of Saint Peter, to meditate
and pray.

Louis XVI. did not think it right to oppose his

aunts' desire. Their passports were signed, and Cardinal de Bernis, the French Ambassador to Rome, was notified of their speedy arrival. They were about to start, when, on February 3, 1791, an anonymous intimation of their intention was sent to the Jacobin Club. Alarm, fury against the court, patriotic rage, was the immediate result. A deputation from the municipal body went to the Assembly and to the Tuileries to make complaint. "I have already explained to the municipality," said Louis XVI., "that my aunts, being their own mistresses, have the right to go wherever they please. I know their hearts too well to believe that any one need borrow any trouble concerning the motives of their journey."

The shrews of the Palais Royal, who assembled in the garden every evening, agreed to go out to Bellevue together and prevent the departure of the Princesses. The ladies, warned of the approach of these menacing hordes, went at once, without waiting to finish their preparations. In the evening of February 19 they abruptly quitted the chateau, in the carriage of a lady who had come to pay them a visit. When the women from Paris arrived, their rage at finding the chateau empty was extreme. They wanted at least to avenge themselves, by preventing the departure of the baggage wagons. General Alexandre Berthier (the future Prince of Wagram) put a stop to this. But he allowed them to enter the apartments, empty the cellars, and loll on the beds of the Princesses.

The language of the Revolutionary journals was a medley of anger and disdain. The *Chronique de Paris* published this sarcastic article: —

" Two Princesses, sedentary by condition, age, and taste, are suddenly possessed by a mania for travelling and running about the world. That is singular, but possible. They are going, so people say, to kiss the Pope's slipper. That is droll, but edifying.

" Thirty-two sections and all good citizens get between them and Rome. That is very simple.

" The Ladies, and especially Madame Adelaide, want to exercise the rights of man. That is natural.

" They do not go, they say, with intentions opposed to those of the Revolution. That is possible, but difficult.

" The fair travellers are followed by a train of eighty persons. That is fine. But they carry away twelve millions. That is very ugly.

" They need change of air. That is the custom. But this removal disturbs their creditors. That is also the custom.

" They burn to travel (the desire of young girls is a devouring fire). That is the custom. People burn to keep them at home. That is also the custom."

The *Sabbats Jacobites* used still more ironical language. It said: —

" The Ladies are going to Italy to try the power of their tears and their charms upon the princes of that country. Already the Grand Master of Malta has caused Madame Adelaide to be informed that he

will give her his heart and hand as soon as she has
quitted France, and that she may count upon the
assistance of three galleys and forty-eight cavaliers,
young and old. Our Holy Father undertakes to
marry Victoire and promises her his army of three
hundred men to bring about a counter-revolution."

The journey of the Ladies was painful. At Moret
people wished to arrest them, and cried, " To the
lamp-post! " It was owing to the protection of some
cavaliers belonging to the Lorraine Chasseurs that
they were able to continue their route. February 21,
at the moment of entering Arnay-le-Duc, they were
made prisoners by the municipality of the town, who
determined to keep them until the National Assembly
should have decided whether or not they might continue their journey. The question was taken to Paris,
in the name of the municipality of Arnay-le-Duc, by
one of the town officials, and M. de Narbonne, on behalf of the Princesses. While awaiting a solution,
the two Princesses were confined in a miserable
room in a tavern.

The National Assembly discussed the matter. M.
de Narbonne, their chevalier of honor, pleaded the
cause of the Ladies very skilfully. " The welfare of
the people," said Mirabeau, " cannot depend on the
journey the Ladies undertake to Rome; while they
are promenading near the places where the Capitol
once stood, nothing prevents the edifice of our liberty from rising to its utmost height." The debate
was ended by Count de Menou, who exclaimed:

"Europe will doubtless be much astonished, when it learns that the National Assembly of France spent four entire hours in deliberating on the departure of two ladies who would rather hear Mass in Rome than in Paris."

Conformably with Mirabeau's advice, the National Assembly declared that the Ladies were at liberty to depart. At Arnay-le-Duc there was a riot. The populace were unwilling to accept the decision of the Assembly. The Princesses were detained for two days longer, and were only permitted to continue their journey on March 3, after eleven days' imprisonment. When they had crossed the bridge of Beauvoisin, they were hooted from the French shore, while salvos of artillery welcomed them to foreign soil. They could not believe they were in safety until they reached Chambéry, where one of the chief palace officials of the King of Sardinia saluted them in his master's name, and installed them in the palace.

At Paris the excitement had been very great. On the very evening when the Assembly decided in favor of the Ladies, a crowd of rioters, public women, and Jacobin emissaries, invaded the courts and the garden of the Tuileries, demanding, with furious cries, that the King should order the Ladies to return to him at once. The National Guard came up. The gates of the chateau were closed. The populace commanded the soldiers to lay down their bayonets, but they refused. Six cannons were levelled at the crowd. "I

have always wished to display gentleness," said Louis
XVI., "but one must know how to combine it with
firmness, and teach the people that they were not
made to dictate the law, but to obey it." Lafayette
was ordered to disperse the crowd, and he succeeded
in doing so.

XI.

THE KNIGHTS OF THE PONIARD.

THERE is no longer any dike in the way of the torrent. Anarchy is everywhere. The governmental machine is broken. Louis XVI. is no longer more than the shadow of a king. There is no calumny, however absurd, which is not universally believed; no appeal to the passions which does not receive immediate hearing. Words lose their meaning. Rebellion is called patriotism. The faithful servants who come to protect the person of their king with a rampart of their own bodies, are treated as seditious, as assassins, and are pointed out to popular vengeance under the melodramatic title of "Knights of the Poniard."

The multitude is restless, agitated, on the morning of February 28, 1791. One might say that the explosive materials with which the ground is strewn are about to be set on fire. Certain repairs are being made in the dungeon of Vincennes, so that it may serve as an auxiliary to the prisons of Paris. A rumor spreads among the populace to the effect that a new Bastille is preparing, to succeed the former

one. The rioters, recruited from the Faubourg Saint
Antoine by Santerre, go to the castle of Vincennes,
and begin demolishing a parapet, and afterwards several other parts of the dungeon.

Apprised of this popular movement, Lafayette
goes at once to Vincennes, with a detachment of the
National Guard. In the Faubourg Saint Antoine
the people show hostile dispositions, and three battalions of this faubourg refuse to march. But the commander of the battalion of the Capuchins of the
Marais, followed by a large number of volunteers,
penetrates to the dungeon, and puts a stop to the
demolition. Sixty-four rioters, who resist, are arrested.

On returning from the expedition, which has
lasted until night, some men, lurking in the Vincennes forest, fire several shots at Lafayette's aide-
de-camp, mistaking him for the general. Arrived
at the Barrière du Trône, the National Guards find
the gate closed, and the inhabitants of the faubourg
refuse to open it. The cavalry, supported by infantry
and twelve pieces of artillery, are obliged to intervene
in order to vindicate the law and conduct the prisoners to the Hôtel de Ville.

The session of the National Assembly has been
more stormy than usual on this day, and Mirabeau
has resisted the tempest with supreme energy. In
spite of all clamor, he has opposed a law they are
seeking to enact against emigration. " This popularity of mine," he had cried in his voice of thunder,

"this popularity which I have aspired to and enjoyed like any other man, is not a feeble reed. I will bed it deep in the ground, and I will make it germinate on the soil of justice and reason. . . . I swear — if an emigration law is passed — I swear to disobey it. . . . I beg those who interrupt me to remember that I have resisted tyranny all my life, and that I will resist it wherever it may be established."

The day is full of agitation. While the rioters are seeking to demolish the dungeon of Vincennes, and Mirabeau is in the tribune, the Palace of the Tuileries becomes a prey to the keenest anguish. It is rumored that an insurrection is organizing and that it will violate the sanctuary of the monarchy. Several noblemen, carrying arms under their coats, come spontaneously to the palace in order to defend the royal family. They penetrate even to the King's apartments, and Louis XVI. comes out to see them. "Sire," say they, "your nobles hasten to surround your sacred person." The sovereign moderates their zeal and replies that he is in safety.

At the same time the heads of the revolutionists are getting overheated. The nobles who had come to the palace through a chivalrous impulse are stigmatized as conspirators whose intention is to assassinate the National Guards. Lafayette, coming back from Vincennes, goes to the palace, where he finds great excitement. There has just been a brawl. The National Guards on duty have insulted the nobles, some of whom have been struck, and even wounded. Some have been sent flying at the butt end of a musket, some trodden under foot, others rolled in the mud. The Duke of Pienne and Count Alexandre de Tilly are among the most badly treated. Some have opposed an energetic resistance, notably the Marquis of Chabert, chief of squadron, and the Marquis of Beauharnais, a member of the National Assembly. Louis XVI. has requested his adherents to lay down their arms. Lafayette orders them to do so. The nobles tremblingly deposit their weapons on two large tables in the King's ante-chamber. They are afterwards taken to the quarters of M. de Gouvion, who lodges in one of the courts of the palace.

The next day, Lafayette has an account of the affair posted up. MM. de Duras and de Villequier, first gentlemen of the chamber, who had authorized the introduction of these so-called conspirators into the palace, are described in this account as head-servants. They hand in their resignations and leave France. Among the people, the evening of February 28 becomes the subject of numberless comments. By all accounts, the Knights of the Poniard, which is the new name given to the King's adherents, intended nothing less than a Saint Bartholomew's day against the patriots.

The *Moniteur* had at first published a succinct account of the incident. March 5, it published the following declaration of dissent addressed it by a National Guard: "You are making game of your subscribers in giving them your flat and unfaithful account of what happened at the Tuileries on the evening of February 28. What! when seven or eight hundred assassins, ex-chevaliers, viscounts, barons, dukes, and marquises surround the throne, armed with pistols, dirks, and poniards, in order to take by surprise the National Guards, whom they have caused to be assailed from another quarter by a troop of maddened people; when this horde of brigands is joined by a crowd of hired assassins, who do not own to being hired, you say coldly, 'Several private persons armed with pistols.' Several? They came in hundreds. I saw them! Private persons? What private persons except all the *ci-devant?* Armed with pistols? And with poniards, and dirks, and with all those infernal machines which we tore away from them, and to which not even a name can be given, so much have those who invented them refined upon the villainy of their predecessors in this infamous career!"

It was by such fables that popular imagination was disquieted, and the greatest catastrophes prepared. The nobles had no longer a right to defend their sovereign, and Louis XVI., mortified by the affront inflicted on his adherents in his presence, fell ill with chagrin. In the tribune, Mirabeau uttered reactionist speeches. But the monarchy was almost dead, and Mirabeau was about to die.

XII.

THE DEATH OF MIRABEAU.

" IN these stormy times when we, so prodigal of life,
see our days glide by so fast and end so quickly,
exhausted by labor and the passions still more than
threatened by ill-will, it would seem that the conso-
lations of philosophy can no longer satisfy us. . . .
If death comes too soon, it is so especially for those
who have posterity in view, who eternalize the memory of their names by their actions or their works,
and whom death always interrupts in the midst of
some enterprise, to the great loss of the public who
reckon it to their memory which they honor still
more by reverence and regret."

These plaintive lines, written by Mirabeau on the
occasion of the premature death of one of his friends,
apply still more exactly to his own. He, above all
men, was "prodigal of life." One might say that,
foreboding the brevity of his career, he desired to
multiply and concentrate within a few years, a few
weeks, the greatest possible sum of emotions, fatigues,
joys, struggles, and triumphs. Devoured by an activity which was like a fever, avid of gold, of pleasure,

and of glory, intoxicated with popularity parched
by the myriad fires which consumed his mind and
heart, he descended the fatal slope with the rapidity
of madness. His fate was that of most men who
desire at the same time both work and pleasure. For
them pleasure soon turns into fatigue and suffering;
but when their vices desert them, they will not desert
their vices. Enemies of their own repose, they per-
secute and lay snares to entrap themselves. They
kill the body; if they could, they would kill the
soul. A violent excitement, comparable to the last
impulsion of a broken engine, gives them for a little
while a factitious energy. A lingering habit interests them in worldly affairs, of which, nevertheless,
they already understand the emptiness, the inanity.

Such was the great Mirabeau. It was not without
bitterness that he saw rising before him a power
stronger than his genius, than his eloquence — Death!
He suffered because of his interrupted task, because
of the evil he had done, and the good which he could
no longer do. In spite of all the echoes which repeated the accents of his incomparable voice, in spite
of his numberless flatterers, in spite of his prodigious
renown, he felt that he needed rehabilitation, if not
in the eyes of the crowd, at least in his own. He said
to himself, as André Chénier was to say one day, —

> "To die without emptying my quiver,
> Without piercing, without crushing, without kneading in their
>   filth,
> These brutal bungling laws!"

This giant suffered because he must disappear and
leave none but pygmies behind him. The great
wrestler, torn from the arena, regretted the emotions
of the amphitheatre. As citizen, as artist, and as
patriot, he had whereof to complain. So much force,
so much eloquence, so much hope, so many schemes,
all to be extinguished with a breath! The great
man beheld himself dying with I know not what
melancholy curiosity, and he mourned for his country more than for himself. His death struggle, like
his talent, was to be grandiose, pathetic, theatrical.
His life, his death, his obsequies, were alike extraordinary. In reality, he had shone for twenty-two
months only. He was forty when he achieved popularity, and twenty-two months had sufficed him to
make a name which places him in history at the side
of Cicero and Demosthenes.

It was at the moment when he was about to go
down into the tomb that he exerted the most irresistible influence over the Assembly. His voice,
even when he uttered but a single word from his
bench, had a formidable accent. A nod was sufficient to rule his friends and intimidate his foes.
When, turning toward the Barnaves and the Lameths,
he shouted, "Silence, those votes!" the vanquished
and trembling opposition held their peace; but Death,
which makes game of all projects and all glories,
was about to say to the conqueror, "Thou shalt
go no further!" It was when he was most laden
with crowns that the victor felt himself stagger

and fall. The excess of his emotions had slain him.
His head grew heavy, and his gait sluggish. A melancholy, not habitual with him, oppressed all his
being. He had sudden fainting fits. He tried in
vain to arrest the malady by baths containing corro-
sive sublimate in solution. They had no effect other
than to give him a greenish tint which was attributed to poison. Instead of taking precautions, he
abused his strength to the very end. An orgy at the
house of an opera dancer gave the final blow, and on
March 28, 1791, he took to his bed, never to rise
again.

The excitement in Paris was immense. A vast
multitude surrounded the house of the sick man in
the rue Chaussée d'Antin. Bulletins of his condition
were transmitted from mouth to mouth to the very
extremities of Paris. His principal adversary, Barnave, came at the head of a deputation of Jacobins
to get tidings of him. Mirabeau loved life, and
struggled against death with all the energy of his
powerful nature. "You are a great doctor," he said
to Cabanis, "but there is a greater one than you:
He who made the wind which overthrows all things,
the water which penetrates and fecundates all, the
fire which quickens all"; and he still hoped that this
Great Physician would work a miracle and save him.
In spite of intolerable pains, he continued to be interested in what went on in the Assembly. Knowing
that a law concerning the right to devise property
had been put on the order of the day, he told Talley-

rand that he had a speech on the subject already prepared, and asked him to read it from the tribune. "It will be amusing," he added, "to listen to what a man who made his will the day before, has to say against the capacity to make one."

He occupied himself with foreign affairs also. "Pitt," said he, "is the minister of preparatives; he governs by his threats more than by his deeds. If I were to live, I think I should give him some annoyance." Even in his death-agony he had moments of pride. He said to his servant, "Support this head, the most powerful one in France." Flattered by the multitude of persons who thronged about him, he exclaimed: "See all these people who surround me; they wait on me like servants, and they are my friends; it is permissible to love life and to regret it, when one leaves such wealth behind him." On the day of his death, April 2, he had the windows thrown open, and addressing Cabanis, he said: "My friend, I shall die to-day. When one comes to that, there is but one thing remaining, and that is to perfume one's self, to be crowned with flowers and environed with music, so as to enter as agreeably as possible into the slumber from which one wakes no more. Give me your word that you will not let me suffer useless pains. . . . I want to enjoy without admixture the presence of all that is dear to me."

Some minutes later, he said bitterly, "My heart is full of grief for the monarchy whose ruins will

become the prey of the seditious." Then speech
failed him. He made signs for a pen which was
near his bed, and with his failing hand wrote the
word: "Sleep." Cabanis pretended not to understand him. Mirabeau resumed the pen, and added
this line: "Can a man leave his friend dying on the
rack for, it may be, several days?" Cabanis assured
the sick man that his desire should be complied with,
and began writing the prescription for an anodyne.
Impatient, Mirabeau cried with a last effort, "Are
you going to deceive me?"—"No, friend, no,"
answered M. de la Marck; "the remedy is coming;
we all saw it ordered." "Ah! the doctors!" continued the dying man. "Did you not promise to
spare me the agonies of such a death? Do you want
me to regret having confided in you?" And he
expired.

The Assembly adjourned on receiving the news.
General mourning was prescribed, and preparations
made for a magnificent funeral. The Assembly
decreed that the Church of Saint Geneviève, transformed into the French Pantheon, should in future
receive the remains of great men, and have these
words graven on its pediment: "To its great men,
the grateful country." It was decided at the same
time that Mirabeau's body should lie beside that of
Descartes in this new Pantheon. It was an apotheosis. For three days nothing was talked of but the
celebrated defunct. The people tore down the name
of the rue Chaussée d'Antin, where he had lived, and

in its place wrote rue Mirabeau. M. de la Place, the
dean of the men of letters, entering a restaurant in
the Palais Royal, a waiter said to him, "Monsieur de
la Place, the weather is very fine to-day." — "Yes, my
friend, the weather is very fine; but Mirabeau is
dead." Revolutionists and aristocrats joined in ex-
tolling his glory. Like Homer, over whom seven
cities disputed the honor of having been his birth-
place, both parties claimed the great orator for their
own. "The day after he died," says Camille Desmoulins, "I thought they were going to make a saint of
him in good earnest." The *Gazette Universelle* related that he had not seen his parish priest; but that
at two different times he had spent more than half
an hour with the Bishop of Lyons, Mgr. Lamourette.
He was regretted by the Jacobins, and also at the
Tuileries. The Revolution had lost its favorite, and
the court believed it had lost its saviour.

Louis XVI. and Marie Antoinette were in deep
affliction. Madame Elisabeth alone judged the dead
man with severity. April 3, 1791, she wrote to the
Marquise de Bombelles: "Mirabeau died yesterday
morning. His arrival in the other world must have
been extremely painful. They say he saw his parish
priest for an hour. I am very sorry for his unhappy
sister, who is very pious and who loved him madly.
The politicians say this death is to be regretted; for
my part, I wait before deciding." Absorbed by the
thought of this death as by a fixed idea, she wrote
the same day to another of her friends, Madame de

Raigecourt: "Mirabeau concluded to go into the
other world, to see whether the Revolution is approved there. Good God! what an awakening he
must have had! Many persons are disturbed about
it. The aristocrats regret him deeply. For the last
three months he has taken the right side, and they
hoped much from his talents. For my part, although
very aristocratic, I cannot but regard his death as
providential for the kingdom. I do not believe that
it is by men without principles or morals that God
wills to save us. I keep this opinion to myself,
because it is not politic; but I like those who are
religious better."

The multitude, however, continued to extol the
dead man as if he were a demigod. His coffin was
completely hidden under a shower of garlands. The
Society of the Friends of the Constitution resolved
to wear mourning for eight days, and to resume it
annually on April 2, and to have a marble bust of
him executed, on the pedestal of which should be
inscribed the celebrated saying: "Go and tell those
who sent you that we are here by the will of the
people, and that we will not depart save by force of
bayonets."

It was related that, during the illness of the
deceased, a youth came to offer the transfusion of
his blood to rejuvenate and freshen that of the sick
man. People said also that his secretary, who had
several times drawn the sword in his defence, was
unwilling to survive him, and was going to cut his

throat. On the day of the funeral, Monday, April 4,
some fashionable society women were complaining of
the dust, and saying that the municipality would
have done well to have the boulevard sprinkled.
" They counted on our tears " responded a fishwoman.

Never was there a ceremony more grandiose or
lugubrious. The procession began to form at five in
the evening. A detachment of the National Guard
cavalry opened the march. Then came a deputation
from the Invalides chosen from among the veterans
most severely mutilated; Lafayette and his staff; a
deputation from the sixty battalions; the Hundred-
Swiss; the provost guards; the military band playing
funereal music, and with its drums muffled in black
crape. The clergy preceded the corpse. It was at
first intended to put the coffin in a hearse, but the
battalion of La Grange Batelière, which Mirabeau
had commanded, asked and obtained the honor of
carrying it with their own arms. A civic crown
was substituted for the feudal insignia, the count's
coronet, and the coat-of-arms. Behind the body
walked the whole National Assembly, escorted by
the battalion of veterans and that of the children.
Then came the magistrates and all the clubs.

The procession, which was three miles long,
marched slowly between two ranks of National
Guards. It took three hours to reach Saint Eustache.
At the moment of removing the corpse, twenty thousand men fired a simultaneous discharge. The windows were broken. It seemed as though the church

was going to fall in upon the coffin. After the office
for the dead, the line of march was resumed again
in the direction of the Pantheon. It was midnight
when they reached it. The torches shone amid the
gloom like so many unreal, fantastic lights. Mirabeau's body was placed in the same vault as that of
Descartes. Then the crowds dispersed, and nothing
troubled any longer the calmness of the night.

And now let us leave the word to Camille Desmoulins, who has described this great funereal pomp.
In number 72 of his *Révolutions de France et de
Brabant*, he writes: "Admiration was felt on all
sides, and sorrow nowhere. The honors due to Mirabeau's genius were paid him; but those which belong
only to virtue cannot be usurped. There was a hundred times more grief at Loustalot's lonely funeral
than in this league-long procession. One must tell
the truth. This ceremony was more like the translation of Voltaire, of a great man who had been dead
ten years, than that of one recently deceased. The
refusal of a single man, a Cato or a Pétion, to be
present at his funeral or wear mourning for him,
does more injury to his memory than four hundred
thousand spectators can do it honor. How many
say to themselves at the sight of so much homage :
Mind and talent, then, are all. And thou, Virtue,
since thou art but a phantom, Brutus may thrust
himself through with his own sword, and the victory
of the Cæsar is assured!"

Yes, it is Cæsar who will triumph, the unknown

Cæsar, Cæsar the Corsican. O foresight of this world, of how little account are you! O vaunted geniuses, great politicians, great orators, great statesmen, what can you do against the mysterious future? How brief you are, O human wisdom, and how blind, and how little even the eloquence of a Mirabeau weighs in the balances of Fate!

XIII.

SOCIETIES which appear the most incredulous are often those where religious questions most divide and inflame men's minds. The revolutionary and Voltairian Paris of 1791 occupied itself with theology in a sort of fury. Both in the salons and the faubourgs, the chief preoccupation was to know what would be the result of the civil constitution of the clergy. One might have supposed that the destiny of France and the fate of all Frenchmen depended on whether the clergy would or would not take the oath. Never had any subject of controversy excited on either side more bitterness and anger.

At the time when Mirabeau died, the struggle had entered upon its most violent period. Anti-religious leaflets were distributed to men gifted with sonorous voices and a certain talent for declamation, who harangued the people with them in every public place. Some of them were dialogues in which odious and ridiculous remarks were made by the pretended friends of the clergy. There were also obscene stories and filthy tales about monks and nuns. On the quays

and boulevards, and in all the public places, caricatures were strewn in profusion, either represent-
ing priests and nuns in indecent postures, or prelates from whose monstrous stomachs peasants were
squeezing out stacks of golden coins.

In the other camp, by the side of sincerely religious
persons, might be seen women who had lost their
reputation, philosophers, encyclopædists, sometimes
even atheists, who had suddenly become missionaries,
theologians, and ardent defenders of the purity and
integrity of the Roman Catholic faith.

Ever since August 24, 1790, the heart of Louis XVI.
had been torn by remorse, a torture he had never
known before. On that day, against the protest of
his conscience, he had granted his royal sanction to
the civil constitution of the clergy. The eldest son
of the Church, the most Christian King, the sovereign
consecrated at Rheims, the successor of Charlemagne
and Saint Louis, shuddered with anguish when he
laid his hand upon the sacred ark. By force of votes,
the national had beaten down the religious edifice.
The clergy no longer had an existence as a political
body.

The sale of ecclesiastical property was decreed,
and the perpetuity of religious vows annulled. The
priests, transformed into mere functionaries, received
their salaries from the State. The covenant which
had for centuries united France to the Holy See was
broken. The Pope's authority had no longer any
weight in the balance. Each territorial department

formed a diocese, and every ecclesiastical boundary not corresponding with a civil one was abolished. Appointments to livings and to episcopal sees were to be made by lay voters, without any thought of applying to Rome to sanction their proceedings. All acts of a civil nature passed out of the hands of the clergy into those of the municipalities.

The priests were obliged to swear fidelity to the new Constitution, which was condemned by the Pope; those among them who possessed no private means had only the alternative of ruin or apostasy. About a hundred ecclesiastical members of the National Assembly, among them two prelates, Talleyrand, Bishop of Autun, and Gobel, Bishop of Lydda, took the oath. All the rest refused it. The entire episcopate, with the exception of these two sworn bishops, protested in the most energetic terms. Religious anarchy soon reached its height. There was civil war in every parish. The partisans of the Revolution threatened with the direst punishments those priests who obeyed the Vatican instead of the Constituent Assembly.

The partisans of reaction said that the Pope was about to launch his thunders against a sacrilegious Assembly and the apostate priests; that the people in country places, deprived of the sacraments, would rise *en masse;* that foreign armies would enter France; and that in the twinkling of an eye the edifice of iniquity would crumble. The unsworn bishops issued charges in which they affirmed that they would not retire from their sees unless constrained by force.

They added that they would hire houses in which to
continue their episcopal functions, and bade the faithful to have recourse only to them. The only subject
of conversation was religion. The clubs were occupied
with nothing but the Church. The same individuals
who, two years later, were to dance in rings around the
scaffolds of the priests, now had no other idea than
to find out what the priest would be who should say
Mass in such or such parish. From the King to the
Jacobins, from the Queen and Madame Elisabeth to
the future furies of the guillotine, there was not a
soul who was not passionately interested in this burning question. It was the cause of all quarrels, the
great aliment of discord. In the same family were
to be encountered the two camps waging war to the
knife.

General Lafayette was on the side of the priests
who had taken the oath. His wife remained faithful
to the others. Madame de Lasteyrie, in her *Vie de
Madame de Lafayette*, whose daughter she was, says:
"The civil constitution of the clergy was a subject
of great tribulation to my mother. She thought it
her duty, precisely on account of her personal situation, to show her attachment to the Catholic cause.
She was present, consequently, at the refusal to take
the oath which her parish priest, the Curé of Saint
Sulpice, made from the pulpit. She found herself
there in company with those best known by their
aristocracy. She repaired assiduously to the churches,
and afterwards to the oratories where the persecuted

clergy took shelter. She continually received the nuns who complained and sought protection, as well as the priests who refused the oath, whom she encouraged to exercise their functions, and to assert the freedom of worship. My father often entertained at dinner the ecclesiastics of the constitutional clergy. My mother professed in their presence her attachment to the cause of the former bishops."

Even in the house of the commander of the National Guard — of Lafayette, the liberal man *par excellence* — the cause of the Roman Church had ardent supporters. Mirabeau, — Mirabeau himself, — who pretended to support the civil constitution of the clergy, was, in the forum of conscience, its adversary. He beheld in it, and not without a secret pleasure, a sort of trap which the enemies of the throne and the altar were laying for themselves. In the tribune he hurled invectives at the priests who remained faithful to the doctrines of Rome, and said to them that "if the Church fell into ruins, it was to them should be attributed the cause." And the same man who used this language wrote to Count de la Marck, January 5, 1791: "The Assembly is done for. Not a single oath was taken yesterday, and if the Assembly thinks that the resignation of twenty thousand parish priests will produce no effect in the kingdom, it looks through strange spectacles." In his 43d note for the court he thus insists on the advantage which should accrue to the royal cause from the decree against the clergy: "A more favor-

able opportunity could not be found to league together a great number of malcontents of the most
dangerous sort, and to augment the popularity of the
King at the expense of that of the National Assembly. To do this, it will be necessary to induce the
greatest possible number of ecclesiastics to refuse the
oath, and the active members of the parishes who are
attached to their pastors to object to re-elections ; to
provoke the National Assembly to violent measures
against these parishes ; to present at the same time
all manner of decrees relative to religion, and especially to discuss the condition of the Jews in Alsace,
the marriage of priests, and divorce, so that the fire
may not go out for want of combustible materials."
So Mirabeau, the great tribune, the idol of the de-
mocracy, the immortal revolutionist, was, if not pub-
licly, at least in the depths of his soul, a clerical !

If such were the sentiments of Mirabeau, what
must not have been those of Louis XVI. and his
family? Madame Elisabeth, who set at defiance so
many persecutions, dreaded the religious one. Her
correspondence betrays, in almost every line, her
anguish as a Christian. Resolved, if need were,
to brave martyrdom, she was absolutely resolved
to hold her own against all the world, and even
against the King himself, if that were necessary,
in order to obey the voice of her conscience. She
wrote to Madame de Bombelles, November 28,
1790 : " How can one desire that Heaven should
cease to be angry with us, when we take pleasure in

constantly provoking it? Let us try, at least, dear heart, to efface some of the offences daily committed by our fidelity in serving God. Let us remember that He is far more grieved than angry. It depends on us to console Him. Ah! how this thought should animate the fervor of souls so happy as to possess the faith! Make your little children pray. God has told us that their prayers are pleasing to Him."

January 7, 1791, the pious Princess wrote to Madame de Raigecourt: "I have no inclination for martyrdom; but I feel that I would be very glad to have the certainty of suffering it, rather than abandon the least article of my faith. I hope that if I am destined for it, God will grant me the needful strength. He is so good, so good!" And on February 7, to Madame de Bombelles: "Ah! if we have sinned, God is punishing us well! Happy he who receives this trial in the spirit of penitence! We must thank God for the courage He is giving to the clergy. Every day we hear new instances of it." March 21, she wrote to Madame de Raigecourt: "We are in terrible anguish. The Pope's brief will presently appear, and the real persecution will begin soon afterwards. This prospect is not of the most agreeable description. But as we have always been told we ought to will what God wills, we must rejoice. In fact, when we know just what we have to do, it will be much easier, because then we shall no longer be obliged to use circumspection with anybody. When God speaks, a Catholic hears only His voice."

At bottom the sentiments of Louis XVI. were the same as his sister's. The Pope had written him, July 10, 1790: "Even if you were disposed to resign the rights inherent in the royal prerogatives, you have not the right to alienate in the least, nor to abandon, what belongs to God and to the Church, of which you are the eldest son." This letter from the Holy Father had profoundly impressed the King. He who had suffered with so much patience the attacks on his dignity as a prince, his liberty as a man, and his prerogatives as a monarch, was unable to resign himself to the pangs he suffered as a Catholic. In order to constrain him to sanction the civil constitution of the clergy, it had been necessary to assure him that public safety imperiously demanded this sacrifice, without which both priests and nobles would be massacred. It is easy to comprehend what must have passed in the heart of this pre-eminently devout sovereign, this monarch who was above all things religious, and who valued his title to the name of Christian far more than to that of King.

April 3, 1791, the pealing of bells announced the installation of the curés who had taken oath to the new Constitution. Madame Elisabeth wrote: "The intended curés were established this morning. I have heard all the bells of Saint Roch. I cannot conceal from you that it has caused me frightful grief." Louis XVI. did not lament it less than his sister. The bells had a funereal accent in his ears. The thing was done. The unfortunate monarch never experienced another instant of moral repose. What anxieties! What sleepless nights! What remorse! The royal martyr wrote in his will these sorrowful lines: "Not being able to obtain the services of a Catholic priest, I pray God to receive the confession I have made to Him, and above all my profound repentance for having signed my name (although it was against my will) to acts which might be contrary to the discipline and the faith of the Catholic Church, to which I have ever remained sincerely united at heart."

This poignant regret was for Louis XVI. the most grievous of his tortures. "Cursed forever," cries Joseph de Maistre in his ultramontane ardor, "be the infamous faction which, profiting shamelessly by the misfortunes of the monarchy, seized brutally a sacred hand and forced it to sign what it abhorred! If this hand, about to be hidden in the tomb, felt it a duty to write the solemn testimony of a profound repentance, may the sublime confession, consigned to an immortal testament, recoil like an overwhelming load, like an eternal anathema, upon the guilty party which made it seem necessary in the eyes of this august innocence, inexorable only towards itself, amidst the respect of the universe."

XIV.

HOLY WEEK in 1791 was to redouble the
religious anguish of Louis XVI. The unfortunate monarch felt the contrast between the troubled
present and those happy bygone days when neither
his dignity as a king nor his conscience as a Christian had anything to suffer; when he enjoyed that
supreme good, peace of mind, and when the ceremonies of the Church and the chants of the liturgy,
instead of causing him anxiety, and even remorse,
gave him only joy and consolation. He regretted
his beloved chapel at Versailles, and the harmony
which formerly existed between throne and altar,
both equally threatened now. He sought for the
priests of former time, and lost himself, as it were,
in an abyss of cares. The offices of the Church
reminded him of his dismal situation. The Crown of
Thorns made him think of his own diadem. Might
not this King, whose palace had become a prison,
apply to himself the words which are said in the
Mass of Palm Sunday, after the gradual: "My God!
my God! cast thine eyes upon me! Why hast Thou

112

abandoned me? My God, I will cry unto Thee in the day time, and Thou wilt not listen. I will cry in the night time, and Thou wilt keep silence. All those who behold me deride me. They wag their heads while they say: He put his confidence in the Lord. Let the Lord deliver him and save him!"

The week began badly. Palm Sunday was a day of anxiety and trouble. Alas! the truce of God no longer existed, even during Holy Week. Discord gave itself not a moment's rest. The Church of the Théatins, which the Catholics had hired from the municipality in order that divine service might be celebrated there by priests faithful to Rome, was invaded by people who flogged a young girl, and fastened two brooms crosswise over the door, with an inscription describing the chastisement prepared for any priest or other person who should dare to enter the church. Bailly, the mayor, had the brooms and the inscription removed, but he could not disperse the crowd. The populace remained in front of the church until six o'clock, ready to assault any one who might attempt to go inside. The same commotion was shown in the royal chapel of the Tuileries. There a grenadier of the National Guard declaimed furiously against the recusant priests who still approached Louis XVI. In the evening, incendiary speeches were made all over Paris.

The King, who was recovering from a rather serious illness, had intended to go on Monday to Saint Cloud so as to enjoy a week's repose and perform his religious duties with tranquillity. Lafayette and Bailly had been the first to advise this step. Moreover, it would give him an occasion to find out just what his situation was, and whether he, who had given freedom to his dominions, was himself a free man. The event convinced him that he was a slave. A rumor got about among the crowd that this journey concealed counter-revolutionary ideas. The King, it was said, had refractory priests hidden in his palace, and secretly received communion from their hands, instead of going to his parish church, Saint Germain-l'Auxerrois. The leaders added that the Bois de Boulogne was full of men wearing white cockades, and that three thousand aristocrats were preparing to abduct the King, who would be among the Austrians within a fortnight. Journalists wrote: "Patriots, to arms! . . . The mouth of kings is a den of lies. . . . A fury hatches her brood of serpents in the breast of Louis XVI. . . . King, you are departing, you are going to put yourself at the head of an Austrian army. But you are too late in setting about it. We know you, great restorer of liberty. To-day your mask falls off, but to-morrow it will be your crown."

On Monday in Holy Week, April 18, at eleven in the morning, the King, with his wife and children and his sister, entered a carriage in the courtyard of the Tuileries, with the intention of going to Saint Cloud. The nobles who were to follow him were the Prince of Poix, captain of the Guards; the Duke of Brissac, captain of the Hundred-Swiss; the Marquis of Duras and the Duke of Villequier, First Gentlemen of the Chamber; and the Marquis of Briges, equerry. As the King was stepping into the carriage, Cardinal de Montmorency-Laval appeared for an instant at one of the palace windows. Some of the National Guards at once took aim at him, and he had barely time to get out of sight. At the same time, other guards precipitated themselves upon the royal carriage with shouts and menaces, pointing bayonets at the breasts of the horses, and declaring that neither Louis XVI. nor his family should leave the Tuileries. "It would be astonishing," said the King, putting his head through the carriage door, "if, after giving liberty to the nation, I were not to be free myself."

Lafayette, who was present at this scandalous scene, made great efforts to get the carriage started, but in vain. Harangues, threats, commands, and prayers were alike useless. "Hold your tongue!" cried some one; "the King shall not go away." — "He shall go," returned the general; "he shall go if I have to use force and cause bloodshed." But the resistance continued, and force was not employed. During this strange dialogue, the Marquis of Duras, who had left his carriage, was standing at the door of the one occupied by the King. A grenadier of the National Guard forced him away from it. At this, the Dauphin, who until then had shown no fear, began to cry, and Louis XVI. was obliged to inter-

pose in order to save M. de Duras from further ill-
treatment.   After fresh efforts, as unsuccessful as
those which preceded them, Lafayette told the King
that he could not depart without danger.   The
wretched Prince cried three different times: "They
are unwilling then to let me go? . . . Is it impossible, then, for me to go? . . . Very well! I am
going to stay."

The dispute had lasted about two hours, during
which the grossest insults had been incessantly repeated.   Unwilling either to set one division of the
National Guards against another, or to soil the thresh-
old of the Tuileries with blood, Louis XVI. left the
carriage and returned with his family to his apartments.   There he found his brother, the Count of
Provence, and, pressing his hand tenderly, he recited,
not without melancholy, Horace's line: —

"Beatus ille qui procul negotiis!"

Shortly afterwards, some National Guards and common people entered the palace, and searched the
apartments, the granaries, the courtyards, and the
carriages, under pretext of discovering the refractory
priests said to be hidden there.

After what had passed on this Monday, no doubt
was left in any mind that royalty no longer existed
save in name.   Never had Louis XVI. sounded so
thoroughly the depths of his humiliation.   He was
unwilling that even his faithful adherents should
longer share his bitterness, and he sent away a num-

ber of them, that they might escape the insults that
were crushing him. He asked the ecclesiastics who
officiated in his chapel to depart. These were the
Cardinal de Montmorency-Laval, Grand Almoner to
the Crown; Mgr. de Roquelaure, Bishop of Senlis,
First Almoner to the King; and Mgr. de Sabran,
Bishop of Laon, First Almoner to the Queen. The
Duke of Villequier and the Marquis of Duras, First
Gentlemen of the Chamber, also received orders to
leave. Marie Antoinette, knowing that her maid of
honor, the Princess of Chimay, a model of piety and
virtue, was daily threatened and insulted, dismissed
her, replacing her as Lady of the Bedchamber by the
Countess of Ossun, who was fated to perish on the
scaffold, a victim to her devotion.

The day was spent in preparations for departure.
The King and Queen suffered profoundly in seeing
their most faithful adherents leave them, and the
little Dauphin, speaking of the revolutionists, exclaimed sadly, "How wicked all these people are to
give so much pain to papa, who is so good!"

On Holy Thursday, April 21, Madame Elisabeth
wrote to Madame de Bombelles: "I will not give
you the details of Monday. I own that I do not
know them yet. All I know is that the King wished
to go to Saint Cloud, and that he got into his carriage,
where he remained two hours; that the National
Guards and the people obstructed his passage, and
that he was obliged to remain. . . . I write in haste
because I am dressing to go to church, since they are

still so obliging as to permit us to do so. Adieu; believe that I will always be worthy of the affection of
those who desire to esteem me, and that, whatever
may happen, I will live and die without having anything to reproach myself with before God and men."

This calmness and strength which are given by
peace of conscience, Louis XVI. no longer shared.
He was about to be forced to what he considered dishonor as well as humiliation — to be present on Easter
Sunday, at a Mass said in the Church of Saint Germain-l'Auxerrois by the intruding curé, a revolutionary priest. Madame Elisabeth could not believe
that her brother would do this. On Holy Saturday
she wrote to Madame de Raigecourt: "It is said in
Paris that the King is going to-morrow to High Mass
in the parish church. I shall not be able to believe
it until after he has been there. All-powerful God,
what just punishment dost thou reserve for a people
gone so far astray?"

The unhappy King, ashamed of this last concession,
sought means to escape from a situation he found
intolerable. Beginning that series of subterfuges
which tarnishes the lustre of his name, and which
a more distinct and energetic attitude would have
spared him, he thought himself obliged to resort to
cunning, the device of the feeble, and by playing a
double rôle, to imitate the example set by Mirabeau.
The secret wish of the constitutional King was to
take back what he had given, and to become once
more an absolute monarch. It seemed to him that

there was no other way to save religion, prevent
schism, and re-establish the principle of authority.
It was not ambition, but conscience, which spoke
within him, and he honestly believed that his duplicity toward men would be approved, protected, and
recompensed by God.

On Tuesday in Holy Week he went before the
National Assembly to complain of the violence of
which he had been the victim the previous day; and
on the following Saturday he caused his minister,
M. de Montmorin, to address a circular to all the
representatives of France at foreign courts, in which
he described himself as the happiest of men and
kings.

At the evening session of the Assembly that same
day, one of the secretaries read this really curious
document. Not only does Louis XVI. profess in it
his adherence to the Revolution, "which is simply
the annihilation of a swarm of abuses which have
been accumulating for centuries through the errors
of the people or the power of ministers, which has
never been the power of kings," but he causes it to
be officially declared to foreign courts that "the most
dangerous of the internal enemies of the French
nation are those who have endeavored to cast doubt
upon the intentions of the monarch," and that "these
men are very culpable or very blind if they consider
themselves the King's friends." It was thus that
Louis XVI. pointed out to popular vengeance his
most intimate courtiers and devoted servants, — the

recusant priests and the nobles of the National
Assembly. The circular, a veritable monument of
duplicity, was received with pretended transports
of delight and cries of " Live the King!" It was
decided to send it to the departments, the armies,
and the colonies; and all curés were commanded to
read it at their parochial Masses.

Marat protested against this enthusiasm. In number 443 of his *Ami du Peuple*, he exclaimed: " What!
all heads turned by such a piece of buffoonery! Will
you always be duped by the traitors who surround
you? . . . The circular is merely the production of
some pedantic academician, some rascally minister
of the court." Then recalling that Louis XVI. had
come on the 19th to complain that he was not free,
he added: " Where did he get the effrontery to
accuse of calumny those who have said he is not
free, when only five days ago he came like a school-
boy to make the same complaint to the National
Assembly?"

The *Ami du Roi* said, on the other hand: " If the
despots of Europe, who are not illumined by the
celestial lights environing the apostles of the Rights
of Man, fancy that they see in this letter itself
a new proof of the captivity of the King and the
abasement of his power, no one can be blamed except those who, by forcing the monarch to become
their echo, will have made it plain that he is their
prisoner."

And now comes Easter Sunday. Formerly it was the

day of joy, the resurrection day, the day of light and
life. Now it is gloomy and sorrowful unto death. The
priests whose functions you are obliged to attend in
the church of Saint Germain-l'Auxerrois, unfortunate
monarch, you look upon as apostates and traitors.
Your sister Elisabeth would not come with you to this
sanctuary, which to her seems profaned by the new
pastor, the intruder, the constitutional priest. Yes;
the priest who says the Mass is a rebel against the
commands of the Church, an enemy of Saint Peter,
a salaried official of the National Assembly. Madame
Elisabeth has declared that she would hear the Mass
of her almoner in the chapel of the Tuileries. Placards posted on the walls of a gallery close to her
apartments have threatened her with the direst outrages if she will not accompany you to Saint Germain-l'Auxerrois. But the intrepid woman did not
allow herself to be intimidated. She is praying in
the royal chapel, while you, the most Christian King,
and your Queen with you, sanction by your presence
the religious revolution. And while the Mass of
Easter Day is said before you in the old basilica of
Saint Germain-l'Auxerrois, heaven itself seems full
of wrath: it thunders, a storm breaks overhead, and
in profound sadness you re-enter your palace, or, to
speak more truly, your prison.

SECOND PART.

THE VARENNES JOURNEY.

I.

PREPARATIONS FOR FLIGHT.

PROFOUNDLY stricken in his dignity as King and his conscience as a Christian, Louis XVI. had come to the end of his patience. The decree of June 5, 1791, which deprived him of the pardoning prerogative, crowned his humiliations. "The King's liberty was taken away long ago," said Madame Elisabeth, "and now they forbid him to be merciful." The unhappy monarch had but one idea left: that of flight. He had long been preoccupied with plans of escape. At first he had been dissuaded by historical precedents. He recalled Charles I. led to the scaffold for having contended against Parliament, and James II. losing the crown for having left his palace. Mirabeau had counselled a departure from Paris; but one which would bear no resemblance to a flight: "For," said he, "a king must not go away secretly, even though it were to be a king."

The time was past for acting in such a manner. A departure by daylight was impossible. In June, 1791, Louis XVI. could only fly by night, like a fugitive, like a condemned wretch seeking to escape. To employ force would have been not merely useless, but danger- ous. Even stratagem was not free from great diffi- culties, although it remained the sole resource.

The obstacles to be overcome seemed almost insur- mountable. How would it be possible to deceive a surveillance which daily grew more rigorous? How escape incessant espionage? How quit the palace, and pass through the city without being recognized and followed? Six hundred National Guards were constantly on duty at the Tuileries. Two mounted sentries were always posted before the outer door. There were sentinels everywhere, indoors and out. They were to be found in the passages between the bedchambers of the King and Queen, and even in the little dark corridor contrived in the roof, where the private staircases terminated. Officers of the National Guard, nearly all of them revolutionists, performed the duties once assigned to the body- guards. Neither the King nor the Queen could go out unattended by a certain number of them. In addition to this public surveillance there was that of the servants, perhaps still more dangerous. Almost every one of them were spies. Marie Antoinette felt convinced that among all her attendants she could count safely on none but her first lady's-maids and one or two footmen.

At first glance, escape seemed absolutely impracticable; but the captives were ingenious. Louis XVI. and Marie Antoinette did not despair, and they prepared patiently an entire series of stratagems to evade their pretended defenders, who were in reality their jailers.

Some of the National Guards, on duty by night and day, slept on mattresses before the doors of the royal bedchambers. It was useless, therefore, to think of passing through these doors. But, happily, there was a door, long since disused, which was concealed by a piece of furniture easily moved. By dint of searching for the place whence they could leave the palace with least risk, Marie Antoinette had discovered that one of her women, Madame de Ronchreuil, occupied a little room communicating by a corridor with her apartment, and which might be utilized for the project of escape. This little room opened into the apartment of the Duke of Villequier, which had one exit on the Court of the Princes, and another on the Court Royal. The Duke of Villequier had just emigrated, and his apartment remained unoccupied. Marie Antoinette procured the key to it. From thence one might hope to leave the chateau without being recognized. There were many sentries stationed in the courtyards, but none at the door of M. de Villequier's apartment; moreover, at certain hours they were accustomed to see many persons leaving the Tuileries at the same time, notably toward eleven or twelve o'clock at night, when the service of the day was over.

The scheme adopted by Louis XVI. was to go to Montmédy, a fortified town bordering the Emperor's dominions and within reach of the fortress of Luxembourg. In case of disaster, it would be easy to take refuge in this fortress, which was esteemed the strongest one in Europe. Another advantage was the possibility of receiving aid from an Austrian army should it become necessary. The Emperor Léopold, Marie Antoinette's brother, had ascended the throne within a year, and had expressed his intention to serve the interests of his sister and his brother-in-law.

The town of Montmédy, like the whole French frontier, from the Moselle and the Sambre to Switzerland, had been placed under the command of an ardent royalist, Lieutenant-General Marquis de Bouillé. His American campaign had won him the reputation of an officer of the first rank, and the firmness he had recently shown in suppressing the outbreaks at Nancy had increased his military renown. The National Assembly feared him, and treated him with deference. Unwilling to be subject to any one except the King, he had refused to hold relations with the Count of Artois and the Prince of Condé. Baron de Breteuil, who, in the emigration, was the secret agent of Louis XVI., persuaded the sovereign that the Marquis of Bouillé was the right man to trust, and was authorized to make overtures to him in the King's name.

M. de Bouillé received these overtures with trans-

port, happy at being able to conciliate his monarchical zeal with the interests of his ambition. A
correspondence in cipher was carried on between
the monarch and the general. Unfortunately, revolutionary aspirations were pervading nearly all ranks
of the Army of the East; and M. de Bouillé could
not count on the fidelity of more than about a score
of German battalions and three or four regiments of
cavalry. At first he proposed that the King should
take the Flanders route, as the shortest and most
secure way of leaving the kingdom, and enter Montmédy from without. This plan was rejected because
the King was unwilling, under any pretext, to leave
his own dominions, as that might give occasion for
decreeing his deposition. Then M. de Bouillé suggested the Rheims route, where there were not many
towns to pass through, and which could easily be
protected. But Louis XVI. objected that it would
be dangerous for him to pass through Rheims, where
his face had been well known since his consecration.
This route was given up therefore, and that of
Châlons-sur-Marne, Clermont, and Varennes settled
on.

It was also agreed that the King should charge
himself with all the details of the journey from Paris
to Châlons-sur-Marne, and that, after leaving there,
M. de Bouillé should take the responsibility for the
remainder. May 27, 1791, Louis XVI. wrote him
that he would start on the 19th of the following
month, between midnight and one o'clock; that he

would go in a private carriage to Bondy, a post-station near Paris, where he would take a double carriage which was to be waiting for him, and that one of his body-guards would act as courier. The general stationed a small army corps under Mont-médy and took care to dispose troops at intervals along the route, from this town to Châlons. The Royal-German regiment was at Stenay, one squadron of hussars at Dun, and another at Varennes. Two squadrons of dragoons were to be at Clermont on the day when the King passed through. They were under the command of Count Charles de Damas, who had been ordered to take a detachment to Sainte-Menehould. Moreover, fifty hussars from Varennes were to be at Pont-de-Somme-Vesle.

June 15, M. de Bouillé received a letter from the King, announcing that the departure, delayed for a day, would not take place until between twelve and one in the night of June 20–21.

The delay was occasioned by the necessity of con-cealing the preparations for flight from one of the Queen's chamber-maids, an ardent democrat, whose time of service would not expire until the 19th. M. de Bouillé was annoyed. He had already issued his orders for the departure of the two squadrons who were to be at Clermont when the King arrived, and now he was obliged to double the time of their stay in that town, which might give rise to sus-picions.

Meanwhile, Louis XVI. and the Queen were painfully completing their preparations for escape. Their principal assistant was Count de Fersen, a foreigner who served France in the capacity of colonel-proprietor of the regiment of Royal Swedes. In happier days he had been one of Marie Antoinette's favorites, and he felt toward her one of those profound and lofty sentiments which have their birth in romantic and chivalrous hearts and fill their whole existence.

Marie Antoinette, on her part, if her calumniators are to be believed, may have felt something warmer than friendship for the handsome Swede. A hint of this suspicion is found in the *Souvenirs et Portraits* of the Duke of Lévis. Speaking of M. de Fersen and his part in the Varennes journey, he makes this malicious reflection: "It was unseemly, on more accounts than one, that on this perilous occasion M. de Fersen should have occupied a post properly belonging to some great French noble."

Marie Antoinette was right in counting on the devotion of this gentleman, who had the soul of a knight-errant. He it was that organized the preparations for departure. As the Minister of Foreign Affairs had not been taken into confidence, the first difficulty was to obtain a passport for the royal family. M. de Fersen undertook to overcome it. One of his friends, a noble Russian lady, Baroness de Korff, was about to leave France and return to her own country. She meant to take her two children, a man-servant and two chamber-maids with her, and had applied to the Minister of Foreign Affairs, through the intermediation of the Russian embassy, for the necessary passport. As soon as it was received, she gave it to M. de Fersen. It was this passport which was to serve Louis XVI., Marie Antoinette, the Dauphin, Madame Royale, Madame Elisabeth, and Madame de Tourzel, the children's governess.

M. de Fersen had also undertaken to procure, in the name of the Baroness de Korff, the carriage to be used by the royal family. It was a very large, double-seated vehicle called a *berline*, which had been ordered from a Parisian saddler on December 22, 1790, and which cost 5944 livres. The way in which it was made was enough to arouse suspicion, for, as the King was unwilling to be separated from his family, and as Madame de Tourzel insisted on accompanying them, an exceptionally large carriage was needed; moreover, various accessories had been provided which were likely to arrest attention. For the rest, it was agreed that the fugitives should leave Paris in a large hackney coach, driven by Count de Fersen, disguised as a coachman, and not enter their own carriage until they arrived at Bondy.

Louis XVI. desired also to be accompanied by three of his former body-guards, who had been disbanded after the October days of 1789. He commissioned Count d'Agoult to choose among them, for this difficult task, three men especially energetic and devoted, and of tried discretion and courage.

M. d'Agoult selected MM. de Valory, de Moustier,
and de Malden, who, at the time of the October
days, had distinguished themselves by defending the
Queen's apartments at Versailles at the peril of their
lives. They availed themselves enthusiastically of
an occasion for still further devotion, and were
secretly presented, June 17, to Louis XVI. and the
Queen at the Tuileries. Marie Antoinette asked
all three of them their baptismal names, saying that
during the journey each would be called by his
own, as it was necessary they should be taken for
domestic servants. They were to wear yellow vests,
in the style of those worn by couriers. The King
gave them detailed instructions on essential points,
and all three swore boundless fidelity to their master.
The preparations being now completed, the fugitives
waited impatiently for the 20th of June, the date
appointed for their escape, and besought God to look
favorably on their project.

II.

THE twentieth day of June, 1791, did not pass
without anxieties. The flight was to take
place at midnight, and at every instant the fugitives
feared lest their intention should be discovered.
Vague rumors were circulating throughout the city,
and at the Tuileries the domestics were whispering
together. One of the three body-guards, who were
to accompany them as couriers, was acquainted with
M. de Gouvion, major-general of the National Guard,
and the confidant of Lafayette, who resided in the
palace. In the morning, M. de Valory made a call
on him to ascertain whether the King's intention was
suspected. M. de Valory having alluded to the
alarms disseminated by the newspapers, M. de Gouvion
replied: "I will wager my head that the King has
not the least desire to leave Paris. He is certain
that no one bears ill-will to his person, and that
when once the desired changes in the government
are effected, he will be more powerful than ever."
M. de Valory went afterwards to the Queen to
acquaint her with these reassuring words.

The moment that he entered, through a small door opening on the dark corridor dividing in two the apartments on the ground-floor, Marie Antoinette said to him: "I thought I recognized M. de Lafayette's footstep. That man frightens me so that I fancy I hear or see him every minute." Apprised of the remark made by the major-general of the National Guard, she added: "I thank you for the relief you bring me; I have need of it. Well! we are approaching the terrible moment. Can we get away from here without being recognized? . . . M. de Lafayette has doubled the guards in every direction." — "Madame," answered M. de Valory, "he has taken this precaution to reassure those who are uneasy, and to quiet the grumblers, rather than because he has any fears himself. I venture to propose that Your Majesty should permit me to see M. de Gouvion again this afternoon. If I find him still confident, M. de Lafayette must be so likewise, and it will be safe to wager that we shall make our escape from the palace without difficulty."

Then the King, coming in, said: "If they suspect nothing, we shall easily get away. . . . You are an officer of my body-guards. If we arrive in safety, you and your comrades will not be forgotten. . . . I shall spend to-morrow night at the Abbaye-d'Orval. The Marquis of Bouillé is awaiting me before Montmédy with an army corps. Strong detachments of hussars and dragoons are stationed at Pont-de-Somme-Vesle, Sainte Menehould, Clermont, Varennes, and

Dun. You will go in advance of my carriage. When you reach Pont-de-Somme-Vesle, ask for the Duke of Choiseul: he is in command of the squadron of Lauzun's hussars which is stationed there; he will obtain an interview for you with an aide-de-camp of M. de Bouillé, whom you will instruct, in my name, to execute the orders he has received." Louis XVI. then gave M. de Valory detailed instructions and sent him away, saying, "This evening, at half-past eleven."

Meanwhile, no change was made in the etiquette and ordinary customs of the court. Nothing remarkable had occurred during the day which might attract attention. At eleven in the morning the Queen went to Mass, and, on leaving the chapel, ordered her carriage for a drive at five in the afternoon.

Madame Royale (the future Duchess of Angoulême) has preserved in a curious narrative an account of her impressions during the hours preceding the departure. "It seemed to me all day," she says, "that my father and mother were very anxious and absorbed, without my understanding why. After dinner they sent my brother and me into another room, and remained alone with my aunt. I have since learned that it was then they informed her of their project of flight." At five in the evening Marie Antoinette went out with her two children and two ladies of her suite to the Tivoli gardens, at the extremity of the Chaussée d'Antin. "During our walk," adds Madame Royale, "my mother took me aside and told me I must not be uneasy about what I was going to see, and that we should not be separated long, but would quickly rejoin each other. I listened, but without understanding in the least what she meant. She kissed me, and said that if the ladies asked why I was so agitated, I must tell them that she had been scolding me, but I had made it up with her. We returned home at seven o'clock. I felt very sad, for I did not comprehend what my mother had told me. I was all alone. My mother had invited Madame de Mackau to go to the Visitation Convent, which she frequently visited, and she had sent away to the country the young person who usually stayed with me."

And now the Count of Provence, the future Louis XVIII., shall narrate to us his last meeting with Louis XVI. It was his intention also to depart that night for Belgium, whence he expected to go to rejoin the King. He came to the Tuileries with his wife in the evening, to sup with the royal family and receive the commands of Louis XVI. The two brothers, who expected to meet again before the week was over, were about to separate forever.

Before supper, Monsieur chatted for some minutes with his sister, Madame Elisabeth, who had been informed of the proposed flight only that afternoon. "I found her tranquil," says the Count of Provence, "submissive to the will of God; satisfied, but not manifesting extravagant joy, — in a word, as calm as if she had known about the project for a year. We embraced each other most affectionately. Afterwards, she said to me: 'Brother, you are religious; let me give you a little picture. It can bring you nothing but good luck.' I accepted it, as may easily be believed, with as much pleasure as gratitude. We talked for some time about the great enterprise, and, without allowing myself to be blinded by my tenderness, I must say that it would be impossible to reason with more coolness and judgment than she displayed. I could not avoid admiring her."

Afterwards, the Count of Provence went down to the apartment of the Queen. As he embraced her with great effusion, "Take care not to unnerve me," said Marie Antoinette; "I would not like any one to see that I have been crying." The Prince and his wife took supper with the King, the Queen, and Madame Elisabeth. Neither of them suspected that it was the last meal they were to eat together. All five remained in conversation until nearly eleven o'clock. When the moment to separate had come, Louis XVI., who had not yet informed his brother to what place he was going, now said that he was bound for Montmédy, and directed Monsieur to repair to Longwy, by way of Lower Austria. The brothers then bade each other farewell, in the hope of rejoining each other in a place of safety within four days.

The moment of departure was approaching. After all, the day had passed very well. There had been no denunciation and no grave suspicions. The King received the usual visitors in his bedroom. The ordinary ways of the palace had been scrupulously observed. Orders for the next day were given to the servants. Doors were closed and locked. The lights were put out. The members of the royal family had gone to bed. A few minutes later they got up again.

III.

THE DEPARTURE.

THE moment of departure had arrived. The fugitives were not to leave the Tuileries all together. It was arranged that the Dauphin and his sister, accompanied by Madame de Tourzel, should go first. A few moments later, the King, the Queen, and Madame Elisabeth would leave the palace one by one.

Toward ten o'clock, while the Count and Countess of Provence were still at the Tuileries, the Queen went to her daughter's room, and bade her get ready. She dressed her in a brown chintz frock, which had cost ninety cents. The first chambermaid of the young Princess, Madame Brunier, was in the room, and Marie Antoinette told her what was about to happen. "I would like," said she, "to have you go with us. But since you have your husband, you may remain." Madame Brunier did not hesitate a moment in responding that she would follow the Queen wherever she went. It was settled that both she and Madame de Neuville, first chambermaid to the Dauphin, should be of the party, and that they should set off at once, in a special carriage, and rejoin the royal family at Bondy.

Marie Antoinette went from her daughter's room to that of her son, to awaken him. "Get up," she said to him; "you are going to a place of war, where you will command your regiment." At these words, the child sprang out of bed, saying, "Quick, quick! Let us hurry. Give me my sabre and my boots, and let us go." What they gave him was neither boots nor a sabre, but a little girl's dress, a frock and bonnet, which the governess of the royal children, Madame de Tourzel, had prepared, in expectation of circumstances which might render a disguise necessary. The passport to be used by the fugitives stated that Madame de Korff was accompanied by her two daughters. It was necessary, therefore, that the Dauphin should be considered the sister of Madame Royale. "They dressed my brother as a little girl," says this Princess, in her account of the journey. "He was charming. As he had fallen asleep, he did not know what happened. I asked him what he thought was going to be done. He said he thought there was to be a comedy, because we were disguised." A strange comedy, in fact, which was to end by a terrible drama!

The two children and their governess, Madame de Tourzel, passed out through the apartment of the Duke of Villequier. In front of the palace there were three courts: that of the Switzers, in front of the Pavilion of Marsan; the Royal Court, in front

of the Pavilion of the Centre; and the Court of the
Princes, in front of the Pavilion of Flora. The
apartment of M. de Villequier had a door by which
one could go down into the latter court, and as it
had been empty since the Duke emigrated, no sentry
was now posted there. Marie Antoinette wished to
superintend in person the departure of her children.
She went with them into the Court of the Princes,
running a great risk thereby, as Madame Royale has
remarked in her narration. A large hackney coach was
standing in the middle of the court, with M. de Fersen on the box, disguised as a coachman. This coach
was to take the children to the Barrière de Clichy,
where the berlin intended for the journey was to
await them. The Dauphin, his sister, and Madame
de Tourzel got into the carriage, and the Queen went
back into the palace. The coach passed out of the
Court of the Princes, and went through the rue Saint
Honoré to the Little Carrousel, opposite the house
called the Hôtel de Guaillarbois, near the rue de
l'Echelle and the rue Saint Nicaise. They were to be
rejoined at this point by the King and Queen and
Madame Elisabeth, who were to leave the Tuileries
separately, and on foot.

Meanwhile, the King had just held his reception,
and gone to bed with all the usual ceremony. He
had risen again immediately. He had disguised himself with a wig, and put on the costume in which
he expected to pass himself off as M. Durand, the
Baroness de Korff's steward. Accompanied by M. de

Valory he went quietly out of the palace by the principal door, that of the Pavilion of the Centre. The sentries did not recognize him. He was supposed to be one of the numerous persons who left the Tuileries every night toward twelve o'clock, after the King had gone to bed.

The Queen and Madame Elisabeth went out, one after the other, through the door of M. de Villequier's apartment. Marie Antoinette wore a sort of brown tunic, a black hat in the Chinese style, ornamented with a long piece of lace which answered for a veil. M. de Moustier gave her his arm; Madame Elisabeth was attended by M. de Malden.

All this time the coach containing the Dauphin, his sister, and their governess, was standing in the Little Carrousel, in front of the Hôtel de Guaillarbois. "My brother," says Madame Royale, "was lying in the bottom of the carriage, under Madame de Touzel's gown. We saw M. de Lafayette pass, returning from my father's bedchamber. We were waiting there at least an hour, without knowing what had happened. Never has any time seemed to me so long. . . . At last, at the end of an hour, I saw a woman walking around the carriage. I was afraid that we had been discovered, but I was reassured by seeing the coachman open the door. It was my aunt."

A few minutes later Louis XVI. arrived. There was no one missing now except the Queen. Each minute of delay caused the fugitives inexpressible anguish. They said to each other that Marie Antoinette had doubtless been recognized, and as they would not on any account start without her, they thought they would be obliged to abandon their journey.

The Queen had not been recognized, but she had lost her way. The vast space which separates the Tuileries from the Louvre, and which is now one of the most beautiful spots in Europe, was then a laby-rinth where numerous streets crossed each other, the Carrousel, Saint Nicaise, Rohan, Chartres, Saint Thomas du Louvre, des Orties, and others.

The Queen was bewildered in this maze. She had just been greatly alarmed by seeing the carriage of General Lafayette, who was coming from the Tui-leries where he had made his rounds after being pres-ent in the King's bedchamber. The apparition of a ghost would not have frightened Marie Antoinette more. Several lackeys surrounded the carriage, hold-ing lighted torches which shed so much light that the fugitive, persuaded that the General was about to recognize her, quitted M. de Moustier's arm in dis-may, and fled in a different direction. M. de Moustier tried to reassure her by pointing out that the torches, placed between her and M. de Lafayette, must dazzle the latter's eyes, and prevent his recognition of her.

In her terror, the Queen mistook her way and got lost among the streets surrounding the Carrousel. She turned to the left instead of the right, and went toward the Pont Royal: the night was dark, and she did not know whither she was going. M. de

Moustier could neither guide her nor find the way
himself. They were obliged to ask the sentry on
the bridge, and then retrace their steps, pass the
wickets beside the river, go along the Court of
the Princes, the Court Royal, and the Court of the
Switzers, in order to arrive finally at the corner of
the rue de l'Echelle, where the hackney-coach containing the other fugitives was still standing before
the Hôtel Guaillarbois.

Reunited at last after so much anguish, they offered
thanks to Divine Providence. The coach door was
closed. M. de Fersen whipped up his horses and
gained the Barrière de Clichy, where they were to
find the three body-guards, and the berlin in which
their journey was to be accomplished.

It was the shortest night of the year, and day
had already begun to break. It was about two
o'clock. At first there was some difficulty in finding
the place where the berlin was to be, and Louis
XVI. got out of the coach, to the great uneasiness
of his family. At last M. de Fersen came up with
it. The doors of the two vehicles were placed side
by side, and the fugitives passed from one to the
other. The hackney-coach was left beside the road
with no one to watch it. The berlin was drawn by
five horses. One of M. de Fersen's servants acted
as postilion, M. de Fersen and two of the body-
guards, MM. de Moustier and de Malden, mounted
the coachman's box. M. de Valory had gone ahead
on horseback to order relays at Bondy. "Come on,

now, be bold! drive fast!" cried M. de Fersen to the postilion.

The horses galloped at full speed. Bondy was quickly reached and the horses changed. Here M. de Fersen took his leave of the royal family. He was to start for Brussels the next day, but he wished first to re-enter Paris, so as to assure himself whether the flight had yet been discovered. When he arrived, in broad daylight, he went to the Hôtel de Ville, the mayor's office, and the staff-office of the National Guard. Everything was quiet in these three places; he concluded, therefore, that nothing had thus far been suspected. Meanwhile, Louis XVI. and his family were quietly continuing their route, and the journey, which was to end so badly, began well.

IV.

JUNE TWENTIETH, 1791, IN PARIS.

IN Paris, the night of June 20–21 had passed very quietly. Nobody suspected that the King was no longer in his capital, and even at the Tuileries there were neither doubts nor misgivings. According to his usual custom, the Dauphin's physician entered the apartment of the young Prince toward seven o'clock in the morning to see how he was getting on. He found his room empty. He passed into the apartment of Madame Royale, where he supposed the Prince might be. Seeing neither the sister nor the brother, he began to be uneasy. The alarm spread. It was discovered that the chambers of the King, the Queen, and Madame Elisabeth were likewise deserted. A message was sent immediately to M. de Lafayette, who was at first unwilling to believe it. The news spread through Paris very quickly. The tocsin was sounded. The drums beat the general alarm. The people, believing themselves betrayed, flocked around the Tuileries, the Hôtel de Ville, and the National Assembly. Lafayette, who had gone in all haste to the palace, and afterwards to the Assembly,

144

was assailed as he passed by men who threatened to kill him. Meanwhile, the Assembly had just met. It was presided over by Alexandre de Beauharnais, husband of the future Empress Josephine. He announced the flight of the royal family. The Assembly, calm and grave, took all necessary measures without delay. The Ministers were summoned, and couriers sent to the departments, with orders directing all public functionaries, National Guards, and troops of the line to arrest any persons leaving the kingdom. M. de Laporte, intendant of the civil list, sent to the President a proclamation which Louis XVI. had left behind him, and which was read to the Assembly.

"Frenchmen!" said the Sovereign, "do you desire that anarchy and the despotism of the clubs should replace the monarchical government under which the nation has prospered during fourteen hundred years? Do you wish to see your King overwhelmed with outrages, and deprived of his own liberty while endeavoring to establish yours?"

In the same document, Louis XVI. enumerated all his griefs: the outrages of the October Days, the inconveniences of residing in the Tuileries, the insufficiency of the civil list, the disbanding of his bodyguards, the attacks made on the rights of the crown, the obstacles put in the way of his visit to Saint Cloud, and the obligation to be present, on Easter Sunday, at the parochial mass of an intruded curé. "Frenchmen! and you, Parisians!" said the King, in conclusion, "inhabitants of a city which our ancestors took pleasure in calling the good city of Paris, distrust the suggestions and the falsehoods of your pretended friends. Return to your King; he will always be your father. What pleasure will it not give him to forget his personal injuries, and to return among you, when a constitution which he shall have freely accepted will have caused our religion to be respected, so that government may be established on a solid footing!"

The Assembly, after having listened to this document, passed unmoved to the order of the day, and continued its discussion of a projected penal code.

M. de Lafayette, meanwhile, had gone to the Hôtel de Ville, in order to concert with the municipal officers and the Council of the Commune means of discovering the route taken by the royal family. Some one suggested that all the hack-drivers of Paris should be summoned. One of them had taken Mesdames de Neuville and Brunier, the two lady's-maids, to Bondy. He had seen and heard a good deal, and it was his report, doubtless, which gave a hint of the direction the fugitives had taken, and decided General Lafayette to despatch two of his aides-de-camp on their tracks. The two officers set off in great haste. The King was a long way in advance, and it seemed hardly possible to overtake him.

Moreover, it was only the people who sincerely desired the arrest and return of the royal family. Their flight, or say rather their deliverance, over-

whelmed the faithful royalists with joy; while, on
the other hand, the Revolutionists, whether republicans or Orleanists, were equally pleased by it. As the
Marquis of Ferrières has remarked in his Memoirs,
" the Orleanists were looking forward to the King's
departure from the realm, and the commotions sure
to result from it, in hopes that the Parisians and the
constitutional party, furious at being deceived, would
be obliged to throw themselves into the arms of the
Duke of Orleans and offer him the crown." While
the partisans of this prince went about repeating that
the flight of Louis XVI. was in reality an abdication,
a legal annulment of the contract between the nation
and the monarch, the republicans, who, although few
in number, were beginning to show their heads,
destroyed the royal escutcheon and monogram on
the signs. They were delighted to see that in spite
of the monarch's absence, everything took its accustomed course, — the artisans going to their work, the
cabs rolling through Paris, and, in the evening, not
a single theatre closing its doors. They said that by
the flight of Louis XVI. France would gain the suppression of the civil list, a saving of thirty millions
a year.

The demagogues did all they could to excite popular feeling, not merely against the King, but against
Lafayette and Bailly, whom they loudly accused of
complicity in the escape, and whom they described as
traitors. Camille Desmoulins wrote in his journal:
" On Tuesday, June 21, it is discovered that the

King and all his family have taken flight. This
general scamper of the male and female Capets took
place at eleven o'clock in the evening, and the news
did not get about until nine the next morning.
Treason! perjury!   Barnave and Lafayette abuse
our confidence!"   Then, to accentuate the charge
more sharply, he added: "I was returning from the
Jacobins with Danton and other patriots at eleven
o'clock; we saw only one patrol the whole way.
Paris appeared to me so deserted that I could not
avoid remarking on it.   One of us, who had a letter
in his pocket, warning him that the King was to
depart that night, wanted to watch the palace; he
saw M. de Lafayette enter it at eleven o'clock."
Finally, in a paroxysm of anger, Camille Desmoulins
exclaimed: "As the King animal is an aliquot part
of the human species, and as we have had the folly
to make him an integral part of the body politic, he
must be subjected to the laws of society, which have
ordained that any man who takes arms against the
nation shall be punished with death, and to the laws
of the human species, the natural law, which permits
one to kill an enemy who attacks him.   Now, the
King has taken aim at the nation.   It is true his gun
hung fire, but it is the nation's turn to shoot."

At the Cordeliers club, Danton uttered this famous
invective against Lafayette: "You swore that the
King should not depart; you made yourself his
surety.   Of two things, one: either you are a traitor
who has betrayed his country, or you are stupid in

having made yourself answerable for a person for whom you could not answer. In the most favorable case you have proved yourself incapable of commanding us. I descend from the tribune; I have said enough to demonstrate that if I despise traitors, I do not fear assassins."

Meanwhile, the mass of the people, who were neither Orleanist nor republican, seemed profoundly afflicted by the departure of the royal family, and ardently desirous of their return. They said to each other that if the King did not come back, civil war would break out, foreigners would invade France, and Paris would be given over to blood and fire. People got excited. News was awaited with feverish impatience. While this anxiety troubled the inhabitants of Paris, Louis XVI. and his family were quietly pursuing their journey. "Here I am then," said the fugitive King, "outside of that city of Paris where I have tasted so much bitterness! By this time, Lafayette ought to be a good deal embarrassed about his own safety."

V.

THE JOURNEY.

THE six-horse carriage containing the royal family went on all day without encountering any obstacles. M. de Valory preceded it as courier; MM. de Malden and de Moustier were on the box, and Mesdames de Neuville and Brunier followed in a post-chaise. Madame de Tourzel passed for the Baroness de Korff, and the Queen for Madame Rochet, governess to the daughters of that lady. The Dauphin and his sister were styled Amélie and Aglaé, the two daughters of the baroness; Madame Elisabeth was their nurse; the King played the part of Mr. Durand, a steward; the three body-guards were men-servants. M. de Valory was addressed as François; M. de Malden, as Saint-Jean; M. de Moustier as Melchior. The travellers did not even stop to eat, having all necessary provisions in the carriage. Their passport was not asked for, and no one made any difficulty about supplying them with horses.

At the post-station of Jalon, which was the last before reaching Châlons-sur-Marne, the Queen said to M. de Valory : "François, it seems to me that everything is going very well; we should be arrested by this time if we are going to be; they have not yet noticed our departure." "Madame," replied M. de Valory, "as soon as we were twelve leagues away from Paris, all cause for anxiety was over. We should have been stopped before we got so far if anything had been discovered after the visit to the King's bedchamber, or our departure from the palace. There is no reason for alarm. I have seen no commotion or suspicion anywhere. Take courage, Madame; all is going well." The King, for his part, said: " When we have passed Châlons, we shall have nothing more to fear; at Pont-de-Somme-Vesle we shall find the first detachment of troops, and our journey is safe." They arrived at Châlons at about four in the afternoon. The greatest quiet reigned there. They left without difficulty, after changing horses.

At Châlons-sur-Marne ended the arrangements which were undertaken by the King and Queen. The Marquis de Bouillé had made himself responsible for the remainder of the journey.

The royal family were to make the following halting-places: Pont-de-Somme-Vesle, three leagues from Châlons; Sainte Menehould, four leagues from Pont-de-Somme-Vesle; Clermont-en-Argonne, four leagues from Sainte Menehould; Varennes, three leagues from Clermont-en-Argonne; Dun, five leagues from Varennes; and, five leagues from Dun, Montmédy. It had been arranged that at each of these stations there would be a detachment of cavalry.

The orders of the Marquis de Bouillé were such that if the King wished to make himself known to his troops, the detachments which had formed his escort would, at each new post, fall back behind his carriage to form a rear-guard, giving place to the fresh detachments found there, which would act as vanguard. If, on the contrary, His Majesty desired to preserve his incognito, the detachments which were to escort him should allow the carriage to go ahead, so as to give time for the exchange of horses, taking care, however, to march close behind, so as to avert all accidents. Their orders were to follow the carriage exactly, forming an impenetrable barrier, through which no courier or other person should pass on any pretext whatever, and to arrive all together and at the same time with the King, at Montmédy, which had been provisioned for the support of a numerous army during several months.[1]

It was at Pont-de-Somme-Vesle that Louis XVI. expected to find the first detachment, under command of the Duke de Choiseul, nephew of the celebrated minister of Louis XV., and colonel of the regiment of Royal Dragoons. According to the plan of the Marquis de Bouillé, it was from this point that the orders for the succeeding stations were to issue. The royal family reached Pont-de-Somme-Vesle at half-past five in the evening. Cruel surprise! They found there neither the Duke de Choiseul nor the detach-

---

[1] Account of M. Deslon, captain of the regiment of Lauzun Hussars. M. Deslon commanded the detachment of Dun.

ment of cavalry. " The earth," said Louis XVI. later
on, " seemed to open beneath me." What had happened?

According to the plan of the journey, everything
had been calculated to the minute, and the transit
through Pont-de-Somme-Vesle had been fixed for
half-past three in the afternoon. A delay of some
hours occurring, the Duke de Choiseul became
alarmed by the disturbance his troops occasioned.
The people said openly that the pretended arrival of
a sum of money which needed an escort was a mere
pretext. M. de Choiseul, abandoning all hope of
seeing the royal berlin, so impatiently awaited, and,
rightly or wrongly, believing himself in danger from
the inhabitants of Pont-de-Somme-Vesle and its environs, thought it prudent to withdraw his cavalry
and gain Varennes by a cross-road. This resolution
of the Duke de Choiseul has been severely criticised
by the Marquis de Bouillé and his son. It caused
a controversy between them which lasted until 1822.

The Duke de Choiseul and his cavalry had hardly
been gone an hour, when the royal family arrived at
Pont-de-Somme-Vesle. This first mishap was destined
to render all the subsequent measures which had been
agreed on abortive. Everything was tranquil at Pont-
de-Somme-Vesle, however. Louis XVI. became somewhat reassured on seeing that fresh horses were
furnished without difficulty, and the journey began
anew.

They arrived at Sainte Menehould as safely as if

they had been escorted. But it was there that the
difficulty began to make itself felt. The detachment
of cavalry sent to this town was composed of forty
dragoons, under Captain Marquis d'Andoins, who,
like the Duke de Choiseul, was in the secret of the
journey. The population of Sainte Menehould, who
were extremely revolutionary, showed themselves
very suspicious. During the day Captain d'Andoins
was obliged to go to the hôtel-de-ville to explain the
presence of the dragoons. In the hope of lessening
suspicion, he had decided not to put his little troop
under arms. The dragoons had dismounted and
were walking about the streets in foraging-caps,
when the royal family arrived at Sainte Menehould.
It was near eight o'clock in the evening. They saw
some National Guards, and not without apprehension.
It was the first time they had met any since leaving
Paris. Drums were beating, and the town appeared
in commotion.

As the carriage passed, the dragoons gave the
military salute, which the Queen acknowledged in
her usual graceful and kindly manner. Was this a
mere act of politeness on the part of the troops, or
was it something more? Had they begun to penetrate the secret? Certainly, no one had told them
who were the persons they saluted. This array of
circumstances did not fail to increase the popular
uneasiness. The berlin reached the post-house,
nevertheless, without difficulty. The son of the
station-master was Drouet, a young man of twenty-

eight, whose rôle was to be so fatal to the King. As
they were putting in fresh horses, Captain d'Andoins
approached the carriage for a moment, and said in
an undertone: "Affairs have been mismanaged, and
I am going away so as to avert suspicion." Then,
passing close to M. de Moustier, he said: "Go, go
quickly; you are lost if you do not hurry."

At this moment, Louis XVI. was so imprudent as
to put his head out of the carriage door. Young
Drouet had seen him the previous year at the Fête
of the Federation. He recognized him. To make
assurance doubly sure, he got out a revolutionary
bank-note, on which there was a sufficiently accurate
likeness of the sovereign, and compared it for some
time with the face he had just seen. After that he
had no further doubts. But the presence of the
dragoons intimidated him. At first he said nothing.
The horses were harnessed and the carriage started.
At the same time, M. d'Andoins gave orders for the
dragoons to mount and follow the berlin. It was
this which brought the alarm to a head. The Revolutionists of Sainte Menehould hastened to the
tavern where the dragoons were, plied them with
wine, offered them money, and cut their saddle-girths
in order to prevent their departure. M. d'Andoins
was arrested. Drouet, in spite of the remonstrances
of his wife, resolved to pursue the royal family on
horseback. A quartermaster of dragoons, named
Lagache, an ardent royalist, perceiving Drouet's
scheme, mounted also, to pursue and watch him.

But the latter escaped by plunging into the forests and taking cross-roads.

Meanwhile the royal family were still hopefully pursuing their journey. As yet there was no certain indication that they had been recognized. The slightly alarming signs they had observed were not at all definite. Moreover, they were leaving them behind, and no others occurred along the route.

Towards half-past nine in the evening they arrived at Clermont-en-Argonne. The detachment awaiting them at this town comprised one hundred and forty dragoons, under command of Colonel Count Charles de Damas, who knew the secret of the journey. Let us allow him to recount what happened at this station: "I saw M. de Valory, and acquainted him with the difficulty in which I was placed by the secret disturbance in the town, and the fear that my detachment would be arrested when I gave orders to start. I warned him not to lose time in reaching Varennes, where he could get relays, and go on to announce the coming of the King. During the ten minutes it took to put in fresh horses, I remained at the post-house, surrounded by officers and dragoons, without allowing it to be perceived that I had any acquaintance with the travellers. The King and Queen saw me, and made signs of kindness and satisfaction. Finally, Madame de Tourzel called me; she asked several questions about the road they had still to traverse, and spoke of the children's fatigue. The King spoke to me; the Queen made a sign warning

him to disguise his voice. It is impossible for me
to describe the happiness I felt when I saw the carriage set off toward Varennes."

Count de Damas then attempted to follow the
royal family with his dragoons. But the same thing
that had occurred at Sainte Menehould was reproduced at Clermont-en-Argonne. The population rose
to prevent their departure. "Your officers are traitors," said they to the soldiers; "they want to drag
you to the slaughter; the dragoons are patriots.
Long live the dragoons!" The soldiers refused to
follow their commander, and M. de Damas, threatened by the crowd, had no resource but flight. He
rode off, accompanied by a few faithful dragoons,
saying, "We must get out of this the best way we
can; but no matter, the King is safe!"

As the royal family had been already some time
on the road from Clermont to Varennes, it really
seemed as if all were safe. The distance between
the two towns is barely three leagues. The road is
excellent. M. de Damas reflected that Varennes was
the last station before Montmédy; that Montmédy
was the desired haven, and that the fugitives ought
to reach it that very night and rest from all their
excitement and fatigue.

In reasoning thus, M. de Damas was reckoning
without Drouet, — Drouet, who, with the ruthless
speed of a hunter, was in feverish pursuit of his
prey. On leaving Clermont-en-Argonne the road
forks; the right-hand one is the high-road of Ver-

dun, the left leads to Varennes. As the royal carriage was starting from the Clermont station, the courier on the box called out to the postilions to take the Varennes road. The postilions from Sainte Menehould who had taken the carriage to Clermont heard this direction given. On their return they met Drouet, and were able to tell him what road the travellers had taken.

Who would arrive first at Varennes, — Louis XVI., or Drouet? The history of France, the history of the world, was hanging on that question. On what does the destiny of humanity depend? On the greater or less speed with which a man of the people pursues a carriage. If Quartermaster Lagache overtakes Drouet, or even if Drouet does not reach Varennes until a few minutes after Louis XVI., the King will not be beheaded, there will be no republic, no empire. The face of the world will be changed. The least accident, the least delay, the most apparently insignificant detail, a broken harness, a tired-out horse, a cross postilion who drives less rapidly than usual, a mere nothing, can unsettle all things here below. Drouet reaches Varennes a quarter of an hour before the sovereign, and all is over with the monarchy of Saint Louis, Henri IV., and Louis XIV.

VI.

THE ARREST.

THE travellers arrived at Varennes at half-past
eleven in the night of June 21. Certain expla-
nations will be necessary in order to follow clearly
the successive phases of the drama about to be
enacted.

Varennes, which is built on a declivity, comprises
two distinct quarters: the upper and the lower
towns, separated from each other by the river Aire,
and united by a bridge. At present there is a large
open square at the entrance of the upper town. In
1791 this square did not exist, and there was a long
street leading to the bridge. Between the bridge and
a church, of which the bell-tower alone remains, was
an archway, closed at will by a folding door. Close
to the bell-tower was a little tavern known as the
Bras-d' Or.

The arrangements agreed on for the King's passage were as follows: A detachment of sixty hussars
of the regiment of Lauzun, under command of Lieutenant Rohrig, was stationed at Varennes. As there
was no post-station in the town, the royal berlin was

to be relayed by the Duke de Choiseul's horses and postilions. The horses had been brought to Varennes by a staff-officer, M. de Goguelat, who was to go from there with the Duke de Choiseul to Pont-de-Somme-Vesle to await the King. According to his instructions, M. de Goguelat was to confer with Louis XVI. at Pont-de-Somme-Vesle, and then start for Varennes in the capacity of courier. As he had several fresh horses at different places on the road, it had been calculated that he would arrive there about an hour in advance of the royal family, and would be able to superintend the final preparations for the King's passage through the town.

This part of the programme was not carried out. At Pont-de-Somme-Vesle, M. de Goguelat had done the same thing as the Duke de Choiseul. Seeing that the fugitives were delayed, and believing himself threatened by the inhabitants, he had quitted Pont-de-Somme-Vesle before their arrival, and without informing the Sovereign that the place first designated for the change of horses at Varennes had been altered.

It had been arranged that this relay should be stationed at the entry of the upper town, at a house carefully designated beforehand to the King. But M. de Goguelat had thought proper to change this part of the programme, and had decided to place the relay on the bank of the Aire, in the lower town, at the *Grand-Monarque* tavern. He said to himself, doubtless, that while relaying, it would be better to have the bridge behind him, where a few hussars could readily intercept communication and repulse any attack, than to have before him a passage like the archway, which could be easily obstructed. This modification may have been prudent. But still, the King should have been apprised of it.

For additional security, the Marquis de Bouillé had sent his second son, the Chevalier de Bouillé, and another officer, Count de Raigecourt, to Varennes, for the purpose of superintending the exchange of horses, and to await the coming of the royal family. As soon as these gentlemen were apprised of their near arrival by M. de Goguelat, they were to start for Stenay to inform the Marquis de Bouillé.

At the moment when the royal family entered Varennes, M. Rohrig, the second lieutenant, who commanded the detachment of sixty hussars of the Lauzun regiment, had not assembled his little band. Not being in the secret of the journey, he did not know that the King was to pass, but merely supposed that a convoy of money was expected which he was to provide with an escort.

The postilions and horses of the Duke de Choiseul, which had been destined for the relay, were at the *Grand-Monarque* in the lower town. The Chevalier de Bouillé and Count de Raigecourt were there also: they were waiting for M. de Goguelat, who did not come.

Lastly, Drouet had reached Varennes a few min-

utes before, and had repaired in all haste to the *Bras
d'Or*, the tavern close to the archway and in front
of the bridge, to give the alarm and organize an
ambuscade.

M. de Valory had preceded the carriage on horseback. Arrived at this point of the account he published during the reign of Louis XVIII., he thus
expresses his grief: "Here, readers of acute sensibil-
ities, the unhappy friends of an august and beloved
family, ought to stop if they do not wish to shudder
over each line that follows. Yes, they must tremble
with horror to learn that a man could have cherished
in his breast the thought of crime during the time it
took to cross a dozen leagues, and that, without
abandoning his infernal design, he succeeded in seiz-
ing and delivering to their murderers the best and
most virtuous of monarchs, the tenderest and most
illustrious of mothers, her royal children full of the
charms of innocence, and the most admirable Princess
of whom France has ever had reason to be proud.
Pardon me," exclaims M. de Valory, "the accents of
my sorrow! My hand trembles; those fatal images
revive before my eyes!" Then, speaking of the
Duchess d'Angoulême, he adds: "Ah! the sole relic
of a sacred family, immolated almost entire, ought
not to read this recital, made for history alone! May
it never come within her reach! There is no need
of telling anything to this consoling angel of our
misled nation. This angel has seen too much, heard
too much, and shed too many tears; pray Heaven,

rather, to make her lose the memory of all. . . . But let us reanimate our courage ; let us continue if we can."

On entering Varennes, a few minutes before the royal family, M. de Valory had a presentiment that he would not find the postilions and horses of the Duke de Choiseul at the designated place. This prevision was but too well founded.

Alarmed, M. de Valory looked on every side. He called ; no one answered him. He searched the woods near Varennes. He went down into the lower town. Nothing, absolutely nothing. Meanwhile the royal family began an equally fruitless search. Louis XVI. found neither hussars, couriers, postilions, nor horses. What anxiety! What distress! To be wrecked so near the haven, a few leagues from Montmédy, that land of promise, where the royal family had hoped to rise in glory from the tomb of their humiliations and disasters. Fatality! What is the answer to this dreadful riddle? Why are not the sixty hussars of the Lauzun regiment here at the entrance of Varennes? What has become of M. de Goguelat? Where are the Chevalier de Bouillé and Count de Raigecourt, and the Duke de Choiseul's horses and postilions? How are they to be sought for in the darkness? Of whom shall they ask instructions how to get out of this terrible no-thoroughfare? Anguish and discouragement take hold upon the fugitives. Louis XVI. himself knocks repeatedly at the door of the house where the relay had been expected. The Queen also leaves the carriage, and wanders up and down, hoping to meet some one who may tell her what to do. But there is no one in the streets. The lights are out. The citizens are sleeping quietly in their homes.

Meanwhile, Drouet, at the *Bras d' Or*, is profitably employing the time wasted by the royal family at the entrance of the upper town. Assisted by two or three revolutionists, one of whom is Billaud, the future Conventionist, he barricades the bridge with a cart turned upside down, and then places himself in ambush under the archway leading to it. Without Drouet, all would be saved. With Drouet, all will be lost.

Imagine the suppression of a single one of those thousand little causes which may have retarded the progress of the carriage, and Drouet would not have succeeded in his plan, and the royal family would have arrived quietly at Montmédy. A few soldiers, or even a few well-inclined civilians, would have been sufficient to bring Drouet to his senses, to clear away the obstacle from the bridge, and permit the carriage to go on to the inn of the *Grand-Monarque*, on the other side of the river, where the Chevalier de Bouillé was awaiting it with a change of horses. But the King of France and Navarre, the most Christian King, the successor of Charlemagne and Saint Louis, of Henri IV. and Louis XIV. had no one to assist him, and it was before this wretched obstacle, a cart upset in front of a tavern door, that a mon-

archy once formidable and illustrious was to come
to naught!

The royal family, which had re-entered the carriage
after making vain researches in the upper town,
arrived at the archway leading to the bridge, beside
the *Bras d'Or.* There was the pit into which they
were to fall headlong. Muskets already cocked were
thrust through either door, and crossed each other
within the carriage. "Halt!" cried several voices
out of the darkness. "Show your passport! Who
are you?" Some one replies, "Madame de Korff
and her family." "It is possible, but it must be
proved." The passport was shown, and proved all
right. But the rumor had got about that the carriage
was suspicious and must be detained. Torches were
held beneath the King's face. The municipal council
assembled. The National Guard was out. The
tocsin sounded. The procurator of the commune,
M. Sauce, approaching the carriage, said: "The
municipal council is deliberating on the means of
permitting the travellers to proceed. It is believed,
however, that it is our King and his family whom
we have the happiness to see in our town. . . . I
have the honor to offer them my house, where they
will be in safety while awaiting the result of the
deliberations. The crowd in the streets is being
constantly increased by people summoned from the
surrounding country by our tocsin, which, in spite of
us, has been ringing for the last quarter of an hour.
Your Majesty may possibly be exposed to insults we

cannot prevent, and which would overwhelm us with chagrin."

Louis XVI. did not attempt to resist. He did not yet avow that he was the King, but he allowed himself and his family to be led into the house of M. Sauce. The fugitives were definitively arrested. There was no more hope! All was lost!

VII.

THE NIGHT AT VARENNES.

IT is near one in the morning. Behold this vanquished man, this prisoner, this sovereign who is no longer royal save in name, in the small and obscure dwelling of the procurator of a little commune. See him obliged to parley with his rebellious subjects, to plead his cause like an accused person before the court. Sorrowful night, without slumber; full of miseries, with its alternatives of hope and discouragement, with its medley of personages of diverse opinions, jostling against each other in the shabby room where royalty is at the point of death! The town, astonished at the unwonted tumult which has so rudely troubled its repose; ardent revolutionists trembling at the thought that their prey may escape them; faithful royalists who dare not express their loyal sentiments above their breath; National Guards, still hesitating between the monarchical idea and republican passions; the alarm bell, the pealing drums, the illuminated houses, the citizens and common people who wake suddenly and can hardly credit the unexpected news that the royal family has

been arrested. What a spectacle! what undreamed-
of scenes! How unforeseen and strange are the
caprices of destiny! Drouet, who is working in the
shadow, is the actor who plays the sinister rôle in
the drama of Varennes.

Louis XVI. is here what he always has been:
kind, feeble, wavering, optimistic, judging others by
himself, unable to believe in human depravity, hoping
for safety in the midst of the greatest dangers. A
more energetic man would speak plainly and with
force. Louis XVI. hesitates, temporizes, thinks he
may overcome the rebels by gentleness and good
nature. His language is that of a father, perhaps,
but assuredly not that of a sovereign. Moreover, he
is embarrassed by the presence of his family. The
dangers he would brave willingly were he alone, he
dreads for his wife, his children, and his sister. What
he fears above all, and that through kindheartedness,
is bloodshed. He would not sacrifice the life of a
single soldier to save himself or his throne. He is
unwilling that one sword, one sabre, should leave its
scabbard. The illusions natural to a generous heart
cause him to fancy that the revolutionists will re-
pent, and that his paternal counsels will bring back
again a people gone astray. At Varennes he will
continue to hope up to the very minute when he sets
foot on the step of the berlin which is to take him
back to Paris. So, too, nineteen months afterward,
he will hope as he ascends the guillotine, and believe
that some friendly battalion is coming to his assist-

ance, just as, at Varennes, in the house of the procurator of the commune, he expected, up to the last minute, the arrival of the troops of the Marquis de Bouillé. " Perhaps," he was continually saying to himself, " I am about to hear the trumpets of the faithful regiment, the Royal-Allemand." The unfortunate monarch clings to the house of M. Sauce like a shipwrecked sailor to a rock. What he dreads is to be obliged to return to Paris, that city of afflictions and supreme humiliations. Any other destination would still leave room for hope, but Paris means despair. Therefore when he hears that fatal name, it seems to him that the abyss yawns beneath his feet.

He has not yet admitted that he is the King. The people say and repeat that they recognize perfectly both himself and his family. " Very well," cries the Queen; " if you recognize him as your King, respect him!" This speech leaves Louis XVI. at liberty. He throws off his mask. He explains his programme and the object of his journey. For a moment his fatherly accent imposes silence on the throng which overcrowds the room. In touching words he insists on his ardent desire to know the real wishes of his people, and on his firm resolution to do everything for their welfare, no matter at what sacrifice, whether of his inherited rights, his royal authority, or his private interests. He ends by proposing to put himself in the hands of the members of the National Guard stationed at Varennes, to be conducted by them to Montmédy, or any other town they choose, providing that it be not Paris. He hopes he has convinced his audience, and imagines that the National Guard will receive orders from him. He says: " I thank the commune of Varennes for its good intentions, and I accept the escort it offers me. It is my will that horses should be put to my carriages, so that I may take my departure."

Meanwhile the commotion was increasing. People poured into the two small rooms which formed the first story of M. Sauce's house, where the royal family still remained. The alarm bells of neighboring communes were answering the tocsin of the town. Their National Guards also hastened to lend a hand to those of Varennes, where the whole population was afoot.

It was this tumult which informed the Chevalier de Bouillé and Count Raigecourt of the presence of the royal family. They tried to rejoin them with the horses and postilions of the Duke de Choiseul, intended for the relay. Their efforts were vain. The bridge was barricaded, and the people menacing. The two officers were very nearly arrested. What was to be done? They got on their horses and galloped off at full speed to tell what had happened to the Marquis de Bouillé, who was in the neighborhood of Stenay.

Lieutenant Rohrig had the same idea. This young officer, who commanded the detachment of sixty hussars stationed at Varennes, had not been admitted

into the secret of the journey. He believed, simply,
that he was there to escort a convoy of money. He
had not seen M. de Goguelat, who would have apprised him of the truth. Hence, when the rumor of
the arrival of the royal family reached him, his surprise was extreme. He thought he was doing his
duty in leaving his hussars in command of a quartermaster, and going himself at full speed to Stenay,
to warn his general.

It will be remembered that, at Pont-de-Somme-
Vesle, the Duke de Choiseul and M. de Goguelat, at
the head of forty hussars, started for Varennes without awaiting the arrival of the royal family, and their
passage through that place. It will also be remembered that, at Clermont-en-Argonne, Count Charles
de Damas, menaced by the population, had been
obliged to escape, almost alone, and had also turned
toward Varennes. The Duke de Choiseul and M. de
Goguelat, with their forty hussars, and Count Charles
de Damas with a much smaller escort, reached Varennes about an hour after Louis XVI. and his
family. Instead of charging on the populace, the
Duke de Choiseul parleyed with them, and entered
the town by a sort of capitulation. He caused his
hussars to dismount, and obtained an authorization
to present himself before Louis XVI. The same permission was granted to M. de Goguelat and Count
de Damas. The latter has said: "We went up stairs,
into the room occupied by the royal family. The
King, the Queen, and Madame Elisabeth received us

with expressions of the most touching goodness.
My first care was to say that we must get them away
at once, and by force, if necessary. The King answered me: 'They want me to wait until daylight,
and to give me an escort. They proposed to send
one hundred men, but I have agreed that there shall
be only fifty.' We represented to him that the
concourse of people at Varennes, which was small as
yet, would soon be augmented by the entire population of the neighborhood, summoned by the tocsin
which was sounding in all directions. We saw they
had decided to wait. I do not know whether the
forty hussars brought by M. de Choiseul, if reunited
with the sixty already in the town, could, at this
hour, have dispersed the small assemblage; I do not
even know whether the forty, entering at a gallop,
might not have made the people fly, and if a few
charges in the streets would not have made them
masters of the town; but other troops were expected,
which, meanwhile, were far enough away." An hour
later, the hussars had joined the citizens, were nearly
all drunk, and had taken an officer of the National
Guard as their commander.

According to Count Louis de Bouillé, it would
have been better to risk everything than to remain
shut up in a house, waiting for the population of
Varennes to be increased by that of the whole surrounding country, summoned by the tocsin. But
anything that bore a resemblance to an energetic
decision was contrary to the character of the King.

The advice of Count de Damas was not well received, and the unhappy colonel, driven to despair by this inaction, could only bow in respectful acquiescence.

Louis XVI., always credulous, displayed entire confidence in the fallacious promises of the municipality. His demeanor was firm and tranquil. He received with condescension the importunate persons who constantly entered the room and questioned him in a manner not at all in harmony with the laws of etiquette. The Queen and Madame Elisabeth spoke often, and with real dignity. The Dauphin was sleeping profoundly on the bed. His sister stood near Madame de Tourzel.

Day began to break. The tumult increased every minute, and the situation became more and more critical. Toward six o'clock there came a new glimmer of hope. M. Deslon made his appearance at Varennes with sixty hussars, coming from Dun, the station between Varennes and Montmédy. He was waiting for the King, with his detachment, when he learned from the Chevalier de Bouillé and the Count de Raigecourt, as they passed through Dun, that the royal family had been arrested. Not stopping for orders, and listening only to his zeal, he started at four in the morning, and reached Varennes a little before six, having covered more than five full leagues in less than two hours. His plan was to attack at once, and force his way to the house where the King was a prisoner. He had already prepared his detachment by exhortations and promises, when, at twenty

paces from the town, he saw that barricades had
been raised which barred the passage of cavalry.
He obtained for himself alone permission to enter
M. Sauce's house, and he presented himself before
Louis XVI. He told him that his sixty hussars were
at the entrance of Varennes, and ready to shed the
last drop of their blood for their Sovereign; that
the barricades prevented them for the moment from
being useful, but that the Marquis de Bouillé was
momently expected, and that their united forces
would not fail to deliver the august captives.

Captain Deslon spoke with the Queen afterwards
in German, and then took leave of the King, boldly
asking for his commands in the presence of the crowd
which thronged the room. Louis XVI. replied that,
being a prisoner, he had no commands to give. Colonel de Damas said to the captain in German in as
low a tone as he could, "To horse, and charge!"
Somebody cried out, "No German!" and Captain
Deslon went out. Then he sent a brigadier to look
for the quartermaster who, since Second Lieutenant
Rohrig's departure, had commanded the sixty hussars
of the Varennes detachment. But the brigadier
returned alone to say that the sixty hussars were
blockaded in their barracks and could do nothing.
The double attack planned by M. Deslon, counting
on an accord between the two detachments, could
not be accomplished. He remained inactive, awaiting
the arrival of the Marquis de Bouillé.

Even after this cruel night the royal family would

not yet despair. They lent anxious ears to all noises from outside, thinking constantly that they might hear the tread of the Royal-Allemand. But this fatal journey was nothing but a succession of misunderstandings, false chances, mishaps, and delays. If he had been warned two hours sooner, the Marquis de Bouillé could have saved everything. He will reach Varennes with his faithful regiment, but an hour and a half too late. The two emissaries of Lafayette will arrive there before him, bearing the decree of the National Assembly, and the royal family will be forced to resume the road to Paris.

VIII.

THE DEPARTURE FROM VARENNES.

BETWEEN six and seven in the morning, M. de Romeuf, Lafayette's aide-de-camp, and M. Baillon, an officer of the National Guard, arrived from Paris at Varennes. They brought the decree by which the National Assembly ordained the arrest of the royal family wherever they might be found, and their return, willing or unwilling, to Paris. At the moment of their arrival, Louis XVI. was far from having lost all hope. The populace appeared more and more disturbed. Cries of "To Paris! to Paris!" resounded on every side. But the berlin had not been brought up. The King thought he might yet gain time, and flattered himself with the hope that his saviour, the Marquis de Bouillé, was about to come. The crowd, in spite of their revolutionary passion, hesitated to use violence to their king. It was the presence of the two Parisian emissaries which overcame their last scruples.

With hair and vestments in disorder, M. Baillon came first into the room where the royal family were confined, and in a panting and broken voice said:

"Sire, you know . . . all Paris will be cutting each other's throats, . . . our wives and children are perhaps massacred, . . . you will not go any further. . . . Sire, the interests of State . . . yes, Sire, our wives, our children. . . ." At these words, the Queen, showing him the Dauphin, asleep on M. Sauce's bed, exclaimed, "And am I not a mother also?" "In a word, what do you want?" said Louis XVI. "Sire, a decree of the Assembly." "Where is it?" "My comrade has it." Then M. de Romeuf came forward, holding the paper in his hand. Having read it hastily, Louis XVI. said mournfully, "There is no longer a King in France." Then the Queen began to speak. She asked M. de Romeuf how he could have undertaken such a commission, and attributed all her misfortunes to M. de Lafayette. M. de Romeuf said that M. de Lafayette was far from being the enemy of the King and his family. "He is so," replied the Queen. "His head is full of his United States, his American republic; he will see what a French republic amounts to. . . . Well, sir, show it to me, this decree of which you are the bearer." M. de Romeuf handed the decree to the Queen. "Insolent creatures!" said she, throwing it down before reading it all through. The paper fell on the bed where the Dauphin and his sister lay asleep. The Queen picked it up again quickly, exclaiming, as she threw it on the floor, "It would soil my children's bed!"

M. de Romeuf's attitude did not make the same

impression on M. de Valory as on M. de Damas.
According to the account of M. de Valory, the
severity and arrogance with which the two emissaries fulfilled their mission can hardly be conceived.
According to that of M. de Damas, on the contrary,
M. de Romeuf seemed dismayed; his conduct and
his language gave room for the belief that he was
urged on by his companion, that he fulfilled his mission with reluctance, and that he would have been
pleased if the royal family could have escaped.

Meanwhile, M. Baillon was in haste to depart.
The people, feeling themselves supported by the decree of the National Assembly, stamped and shouted.
The two carriages were got in readiness, and threats
were made that the fugitives would be put into them
by force if they would not enter voluntarily. The
King's friends did everything in their power to delay
the fatal moment. One of the two lady's-maids falling ill, the necessary attentions were prolonged as
much as possible. But the woman regained consciousness, and there remained no other pretext for
resisting. Louis XVI., fearing, not for himself, but
for his family, and believing that if he did not yield,
the populace would have recourse to acts of violence,
soon decided to go. "The carriages," M. de Valory
has said, "were brought before the door of the house.
Some one came to announce that the illustrious
victims could enter them. We had to see a father
made to be adored, a King full of love for his people,
forced to obey his subjects; and, my God, what sub-

jects!'" The Duke de Choiseul and Count de Damas
wished to accompany the King and his family on
horseback. But they were arrested and imprisoned
in spite of the efforts of M. de Romeuf. M. de
Romeuf himself was arrested as suspicious, and was
not released until the next day. " The grief which
he expressed to us," says Count de Damas in his
account, " the care he took to exculpate himself from
this abominable mission, led us to wonder why he did
not destroy the decree he carried, and aid us in delay-
ing the departure of the King. I think he would
have done so had he been alone."

It was eight o'clock in the morning when the
royal family left Varennes. An hour and a half
later, the Marquis de Bouillé with the Royal-Allemand appeared on the heights which overlook the
town.

During the early part of the night the general had
waited for tidings with feverish anxiety. He and
his son, Count Louis de Bouillé, had mounted their
horses at Stenay, toward nine in the evening, and
ridden towards Dun, so as to receive news from the
King more promptly. At a quarter of a league from
this town, where their entry might have been too
much remarked, they went down into a dry ditch
at the side of the road, leaving their horses behind.
Count Louis de Bouillé, in a curious memoir, has thus
described their impressions: "I shall always have before my mind that night of long and anxious waiting,
when the least noise, the least movement, according

as it came or went, penetrated our souls with the most vivid impressions of hope or despair. The latter sentiment took almost entire possession of us when day began to break without our having seen any one arrive or received any news. M. de Bouillé, not able to explain the cause, but well persuaded that some change in his plans must have occurred, returned to Stenay, so as to be better able to give the orders necessitated by circumstances. We were a quarter of a league from that town when we perceived some couriers coming towards us at full speed. Our hearts beat with joy, for we supposed they were bringing us tidings of the speedy arrival of the King. But what was our surprise and grief when we recognized the Chevalier de Bouillé, Count de Raigecourt, and, which was most astonishing of all, the officer in command of the detachment of Varennes, who announced to us that the King had been arrested there at half-past eleven the night before, adding nothing else but some very vague details. It was then about half-past four in the morning."

The Marquis de Bouillé could get no clear idea of what had happened. Making a final effort, he ordered the Royal-Allemand to horse at Stenay, and led them to Varennes, hoping that the King might even yet be delivered. He distributed four hundred louis among his cavaliers, and explained their mission in a brief harangue, which was received with shouts of "Long live the King!" The regiment

started at full trot. All along the road they heard
alarm bells ringing and drums beating from every
direction. It was half-past nine in the morning when
they arrived before Varennes. The royal family had
departed an hour earlier. The officers said it was
indispensable to refresh the horses, jaded by a march
of nine leagues at full trot. This observation, which
was but too well founded, the long start which the
carriages had already, the fear of once more endanger-
ing the lives of the royal family while seeking vainly
to bring them aid, the menacing dispositions of the
National Guards and the people, the thought that
four hundred cavalry, worn out with fatigue, could
not but perish in the midst of a revolutionary multitude increasing every minute, — all this determined
the general to give the order for a retreat. "I see
yet," says his son, Count Louis de Bouillé, "the
expression of grief which altered his whole countenance. Never shall I forget that gentle, heart-
breaking complaint which he addressed to me in
sorrowful accents some moments later, and which
alluded to the confidence I had expressed concerning
the success of this enterprise, and based on the good
fortune which had attended all the others: 'Well!
will you say again that I am lucky?'" At Stenay
the Marquis de Bouillé barely escaped arrest. He
was forced to abandon his regiment, and take shelter,
with his son, across the frontier. The latter says:
"We arrived at nightfall at the Abbaye d'Orval, in
the Emperor's dominions. We found the monks at

table, astonished by our arrival, and full of consternation on learning its cause; and at eleven o'clock we terminated that too cruel and too memorable day."

During this time the royal family were painfully continuing their journey, stopping at every town. The fatal Varennes journey had such results that all the incidents of it have occasioned long and bitter controversies. Each actor in it has sought to explain its weak places or its errors; each has sought to shift upon some one else the responsibility of failure; each has said: "If such or such a fault had not been committed, the august martyrs would have been saved." Even yet these discussions interest and excite. The vicissitudes of the journey are followed with as much anxiety as if they had occurred but yesterday. The inventions of romance-writers are not more interesting than the reality; and of all dramas, the most singular, the most interesting, is history. It is not the principal actors alone, but the secondary ones, and even the supernumeraries, who attract attention. All come to life again, all revive, — the characters and the scene. The night of Varennes is legendary. Sinister gleams throw it up into a strange relief. The archway, the bridge, the *Bras d'Or* inn, the house of M. Sauce, all stand out plain before one's eyes, and the imagination rests long upon them.

THE royal family had passed nine hours at
Varennes, and this sojourn sufficed to transform an almost unknown locality into a historic and
forever celebrated town. At eight o'clock in the
morning of June 21, 1791, the berlin which had
brought the august fugitives, took them back again
to Paris. The three body-guards were on the coachman's box. The two lady's-maids followed in another
carriage. People armed with scythes and muskets,
pikes, pitchforks, and sabres, surrounded the two
carriages and formed a sinister escort. At first starting, the horses had been driven at great speed, so as
to put as great a distance as possible between the
royal family and the royalist troops whose arrival
was feared; but afterwards they were allowed to
walk between the constantly increasing throngs — a
revolutionary population. They were four hours in
going from Varennes to Clermont-en-Argonne. It
was three in the afternoon when they reached Sainte
Menehould. This town was greatly indebted to
Louis XVI., who had built it up from its ruins after
a terrible fire. The inhabitants seemed hardly to

remember this benefit. One might have thought
Drouet had imparted to them all his demagogic
passion. Threats, insults, and furious cries greeted
the royal berlin, and the three body-guards barely
escaped assassination.

Not far from Sainte Menehould, opposite the village of Han, and near the mountain of the Moon,
made famous a year later by the encampment of the
King of Prussia and the battle of Valmy, a venerable
old man, wearing the cross of Saint Louis on his
breast, came up on horseback. It was the Marquis
de Dampierre. This old officer, a courtier of misfortune, came to offer homage to his King. The crowd
was not at all pleased with his loyal sentiments, his
respectful attitude, his soldierly and noble bearing,
his white hair. When the old man appeared, the
image of duty and fidelity, shouts of "traitor," "aris-
tocrat," flew from mouth to mouth in the revolutionary escort. "Kill him! cut his throat!" cried
the populace. Some sprang at the horse's bridle;
others sought to dismount the rider. He spurred up
his horse, hoping to make his way through the crowd.
Two pistol shots were fired at him and missed. He
returned them with another. Then he was chased
like a stag at a hunting-match. Muskets were dis-
charged at him repeatedly, and the old nobleman fell
dead. His head was cut off and stuck on a pike; and
the bloody trophy was thrust before the eyes of the
royal family. The horrors of the October Days had
begun anew.

In the evening, they arrived at Châlons-sur-Marne, where they passed the night of June 22–23. This journey, so full of incidents, disturbed by so many emotions and so much anguish, must have resembled a bad dream. The revolutionists who escorted the carriage with cries of fury were like menacing phantoms. The extreme heat, the overpowering fatigue, the moral sufferings, still greater than the physical ones, made this fatal road a way of humiliations and afflictions. That heartrending anguish which Dante places in the midst of his torments — a happy memory recurring in days of wretchedness — came from time to time to deepen Marie Antoinette's emotions. At Châlons-sur-Marne, the royal family alighted in the courtyard of the old hotel de l'Intendance, where they remained all night. The Queen could not behold unmoved this edifice where she had been received at the time of her arrival in France twenty-one years before, in May, 1770.

Then, what benedictions, what transports, what idolatry! With what enthusiasm the charming Dauphiness, the ideal maiden, the morning star, had been received! Who would then have thought that a people so devoted to their royal family would ever become a tribe of regicides and executioners? In a single destiny there are often such vicissitudes and contrasts, that those who fall from the height of prosperity and grandeur into the profound abysses of calamity, lose, as it were, the consciousness of their identity. Unhappy, and questioning the past as well as the present, they say, " Could I have been so happy, so brilliant, and so flattered?" And thus Marie Antoinette might have asked herself in the midst of so many cruel reverses: "Am I truly the daughter of the German Cæsars, the Queen of France and Navarre? Could I once have shone so brilliant, who am now plunged in darkness so profound?"

Châlons-sur-Marne was a sort of oasis in the middle of a burning desert. "Ah! let us breathe awhile," says the Count de Valory in his narration. "At Châlons-sur-Marne a few moments of consolation came to assuage our griefs. But, before attempting to describe this soothing contrast, let us pay to a considerable portion of the French people the just tribute which is their due. Yes, alongside of frightfully barbarous scenes, we often beheld expressive tokens of the grief they occasioned to a great number of virtuous citizens. In spite of every danger, marks of love and profound interest escaped them. One could see it; their hearts were broken, but crime alone dared venture; crime alone was powerful."

The majority of the Châlonnaise population were royalists. They received the unfortunate monarch more like an impatiently expected father than as a king made captive by his subjects. It was who should solicit the honor of being presented to the august family. Ladies and young girls came to offer bouquets to the Queen, Madame Elisabeth, and Madame Royale. Some proposed that the King should save himself alone. A private staircase lead-

ing from the room where the Dauphin slept was
shown him. But he refused to quit his family, and
would not accept the means of escape which were
offered him.

The royalists of the city likewise debated whether
they should attempt to take Louis XVI. back to Montmédy, or to defend him at Châlons. His supper was
served with a certain pomp in a large hall containing
many persons, all of whom passed around the table
without creating the slightest confusion. The emotion was general. People kissed the King's hands
respectfully, and multiplied their signs of homage
toward the Queen and the Princesses. The royal
family were up nearly all night. When they took a
brief repose, the Revolution, which did not sleep,
was preparing to frustrate the monarchical intentions
of the people of Châlons. The National Guard of
Rheims, lead by zealous democrats, reached Châlons-
sur-Marne in the morning.

It was Thursday, June 23, the feast of Corpus
Christi. The King had had an altar arranged, and
was assisting at Mass, which was at the *Sanctus*,
when it was brusquely interrupted by the appearance
of armed men, who summoned the royal family to
renew their journey. "To Paris! to Paris!" cried
voices in the courtyard. Guns were pointed at the
windows, and it was demanded that Louis XVI.
should show himself there. He appeared, calm and
impassible as ever. "Since I am compelled," said he,
"I will go to Paris." Nearly the whole population

of Champagne had marched all night to assemble at
Châlons, and the break of day was, as it were, their
hour of rendezvous. "What could the good Châ-
lonnaises do now?" sadly exclaims M. de Valory.
"Their will was enthralled; nothing remained to
them but sighs!" The royal family got into their
carriage and went on their way, escorted by National
Guards and revolutionary bands.

At Épernay they made a brief stop for dinner.
When, according to custom, the mayor presented the
King with the keys of the town, the president of the
district addressed a sharp remonstrance to the unhappy Prince, ending with these words: "You ought
to be thankful to the town for presenting its keys to
a runaway king." They could hardly eat, so threatening seemed the sentiments of the crowd. Just as
they were setting off, a woman of the city said to
Marie Antoinette, "Go, my little beauty; you will
see worse times than this."

A few minutes later, between Épernay and Dormans, the berlin containing the royal family was
joined by another carriage from which alighted three
deputies from the National Assembly, — Barnave,
Pétion, and the Marquis de Latour-Marbourg. They
had been sent to meet Louis XVI. in the capacity of
commissioners.

X.

THERE are some proud and generous men in whom triumphant sovereigns, with their pomp of luxury and power and their train of flatterers, inspire a sort of repulsion, and yet who instinctively become, so soon as they can gain nothing by it, the servants and courtiers of sovereigns in misfortune. In times of prosperity they ask themselves, " Where is the good in swelling this flood of servility? Why should I add my voice to this concert of adulation?" But the sight of unhappy, abandoned, and betrayed princes inspires in them a mingled tenderness and respect. They do not concern themselves to be faithful when fidelity is rewarded with money and preferment; but when it leads to ruin, poverty, exile, and death, fidelity appears to them an austere joy and a sacred duty. Barnave was one of these men. He had been unmoved by the prestige of success; the majesty of suffering subdued him. Marie Antoinette, illuminated by the reflection of the crown diamonds, radiant in the Gallery of the Mirrors, with her patronizing air, her triumphant beauty, her goddess-like walk; Marie Antoinette amid the refined elegance of the Little Trianon; Marie Antoinette surrounded by the splendors of a royal fête, a court ball, a gala representation at the Versailles theatre or the Paris Opera; Marie Antoinette, on the day of a solemn entry, in a carriage covered with gold, and drawn by eight magnificent horses, would have stirred Barnave's imagination very little. But the calumniated, insulted, threatened Queen; the Queen dressed in the modest gown of a governess; the Queen shut up with her family in the dismal carriage, slowly advancing, like a hearse, on the road to anguish and humiliations; the Queen whose eyes are reddened by tears; the Queen whose locks have been whitened by her grief; the unfortunate Queen invincibly attracts the tribune and transforms him into a chevalier.

Barnave was not quite thirty years old. Born at Grenoble, October 22, 1761, of a respected lawyer, and a noble and beautiful mother, he belonged to the reformed religion. He had early manifested an ardent and lofty soul. At sixteen he fought a duel in behalf of his younger brother, who had been insulted. Impatient of injustice, and penetrated with the sentiment of human dignity, he swore to himself to redeem his caste from the humiliation to which it was condemned under the old régime. Having been made a deputy to the States-General, he at once gained the reputation of a great orator. Full of talent and energy, he held his own against the most powerful antagonists, against Mirabeau himself. In the eyes

of the court he passed for an irreconcilable demagogue, the most to be dreaded among the promoters
of sedition. He who had so often thundered against
the abuses of the monarchy, who for a moment had
made the popularity of Mirabeau grow pale, at the
time when Mirabeau was secretly drawing closer to
the trembling throne; who, in appearing before the
royal family, had perhaps promised himself to stifle
every sentiment of pity in his soul, could not resist
the spectacle of misfortune. As M. de Lamartine
has said, Mirabeau sold himself, and Barnave gave
himself away. The man of genius was bought with
heaps of gold; a glance subdued the man of feeling.

When the three deputies, sent by the Constituent
Assembly to meet the royal family and bring them
back to Paris, stopped the berlin on the road between
Épernay and Dormans, they decided that two of them
ought to enter it. The Queen seemed to wish that
the Marquis de Latour-Marbourg, whose face was not
unknown to her, should be one. Perceiving this,
M. de Latour-Marbourg said to her, in an undertone,
that she could count on him as a faithful subject, but
that it might be otherwise with Barnave, one of the
most influential members of the Assembly. He added
that it would doubtless flatter the young deputy from
Grenoble to enter the royal carriage, and it would be
to the Queen's interest to conciliate him. Matters
were thus arranged: M. de Latour-Marbourg returned
to the carriage which had brought him and his col-
leagues from Paris, while Barnave and Pétion entered

that of the King; the former sat between Louis XVI.
and Marie Antoinette on the back seat, and the latter
on the front one, between Madame Elisabeth and
Madame Royale. The Dauphin sat by turns on the
knees of his mother, his aunt, and his sister.

At first the presence of these new travelling-companions was a somewhat serious embarrassment. The
Queen did not trouble herself to begin a conversation
with them. She drew her veil down and determined
not to open her mouth during the rest of the journey.
Barnave, far from being offended by this silence,
maintained the most respectful attitude toward her
and the King. Louis XVI., who loved to talk, was
the first to break the ice. With the simple and
straightforward manner which befitted his character
he spoke freely of men and things. In his responses,
Barnave courteously observed the fine distinctions
required by the difference of rank, and though he
spoke like a man devoted to liberty and the new
ideas, he also showed himself loyal to the throne,
and unwilling to divorce royalty from the nation in
his projects of reform.

Marie Antoinette listened. She was struck by
the wit, tact, and moderation of Barnave. Like the
woman that she was, she recognized at once in the
manners, the voice, and the countenance of the young
deputy, the attentions of a well-bred man, and felt
herself the object of a discreet and respectful pity.
She lost not a word of the conversation in which she
had at first resolved to take no part. Changing her

mind, she finally began to speak. Her language, like
her person, was gentle, charming, and majestic. In
her voice, as in her glance, there was something
gracious, kindly, and persuasive, which, coming from
the heart, went to the heart. Undaunted by tyranny,
Barnave felt himself vanquished by this strong weak-
ness, this imposing sorrow. His former hatreds
melted in an instant, like snow beneath the genial
rays of sunshine. The idea that he, the citizen, the
plebeian, the unknown young man of two years since,
might by a strange freak of destiny become the support, the protector, the saviour of this beautiful queen,
once so flattered and so brilliant, — this idea flattered
his self-love at the same time that it awakened in
his soul, where democrat and knight-errant blended
into one, the most elevated sentiments and chivalrous
aspirations. Sympathy, respect, devotion, flooded his
soul like a rising tide. Barnave knew well that in
displaying an interest in Marie Antoinette he was
voluntarily exposing himself to the greatest danger.
But this reflection, far from cooling his ardor, made
it all the more keen and fervent. Whatever hap-
pens, said he to himself, I will be the defender and
servant of this woman. Sovereigns in misfortune
easily experience a sentiment little known to them
in prosperous days, — that of gratitude. Then they
prize a word, a tear, a sigh. They recognize, and
thank Heaven, that human nature is not all cowardly, and that amidst so many ingrates there are
here and there honest, devoted, and generous hearts.

Between Dormans and Château-Thierry it was
Barnave who rescued from their torture the three
body-guards who had been exposed all along the
road to the rage of a ferocious population. Some
demons proposed to tie them fast to the wheels of
the royal carriage, and as soon as they were so
bound, to put them to death. They were about to
execute this cannibal-like scheme when the deputy
from Grenoble leaned out of the carriage door to see
what was going on. He alighted at once, and had
influence enough to prevent the crime.

At the entrance of the faubourg of Meaux a similar scene was reproduced. A poor village curé, who
had been so imprudent as to approach the royal
carriage, was about to be massacred. The Queen
uttered a cry. Barnave, throwing himself almost
out of the carriage door, shouted, "Frenchmen!
nation of heroes, are you going to become a people
of assassins?" Madame Elisabeth, touched by this
noble outburst, caught hold of the young man by the
skirt of his coat. The powerful voice of the deputy
from Grenoble availed to save the ecclesiastic from
death. In speaking of this incident later on, Marie
Antoinette said that in the most critical moments
whimsical contrasts were what always struck her;
and that on this occasion the sight of the pious
Elisabeth hanging on to Barnave by the tail of his
coat had seemed the most unexpected and surprising
thing about it.

Meanwhile, the emotion of this new defender of

the throne continued to increase. What affected him in Marie Antoinette was the Queen, the woman, and, above all, the mother. He was permitted to take the Dauphin on his knees, and his fingers played with the child's fair ringlets. "You are not sorry to come back to Paris, are you?" he asked him. "Oh! I am happy everywhere," answered the future Louis XVII., "provided I am with my father, and mamma Queen . . . and with my aunt, my sister, and Madame de Tourzel." "It is a sad journey for my children, sir," said Louis XVI. "What a difference between this one and that we made to Cherbourg! At that time calumny had not yet led public opinion astray. . . . They may misunderstand me, but they shall not change me; love for my people will always remain the first need of my heart, as it is the first of my duties." The Dauphin took his father's hand and kissed it. Then the good Louis XVI. embraced his son tenderly, calling him as of old, "My dear little Norman!" "Don't be sad, father," said the child, who was crying. "Another time we will go to Cherbourg."

Profoundly touched, Barnave redoubled his oblig- ing attentions. Throughout the journey he was a model of delicacy, courtesy, and respect, and he made the most favorable impression on Madame Elisabeth as well as on the Queen. Three months later on, after the discussion of the Assembly on the colonies, the pious sister of Louis XVI. wrote to Madame de Raigecourt: "Barnave spoke with so much force that

he carried all before him. That man has great intel-
ligence and talent; he might have been a great man
if he had chosen; he may be so yet. But the anger
of Heaven is not yet all spent. How should it be?
What are we doing to appease it?"

Madame Elisabeth was right. The Divine wrath
was not yet exhausted. Barnave was to be sacrificed
almost at the same time as the royal victims to whom
he so generously devoted himself. He was arrested
as a suspected royalist August 19, 1792, and remained more than a year in prison before mounting
the scaffold whereon he was to die at the age of
thirty-two. His works, published by M. Bérenger
of Drôme, exhibit fully the elevation of his mind
and the true nobility of his heart. A captive, he
remembered with emotion the journey which had
left such profound traces in his soul; and in speaking of this touching and critical time, he said that
by graving on his imagination the memorable example of the royal misfortunes, it had doubtless aided
him to support his own more easily.

Transferred from the prisons of Dauphiny to Paris,
in November, 1793, to be judged, or, rather, to be
assassinated by the revolutionary tribunal, Barnave,
while on the way, addressed a letter to one of his
sisters, which is like the testament of his soul, where
stoicism and tenderness went hand in hand. " I am
still young," he wrote, " and yet I have already
known, already experienced, all the good and all the
evil which make up human life. Endowed with a

vivid imagination, I long believed in chimeras; but I am undeceived, and at the moment when I am about to quit life, the only things I regret are friendship (no one can flatter himself with having tasted its sweetness more deeply than I) and the cultivation of the mind, the habit of which has often delightfully occupied my days."

Barnave is the André Chénier of politics. Like the young poet, the young orator could say, putting his hand to his forehead, "And yet, there was something there!" A veil of melancholy and sadness covers the destiny of each. It is genius extinguished at its dawning; it is youth which succumbs before having gathered all its harvest of talent and of glory. Barnave died the victim of his chivalrous devotion to Marie Antoinette. He did not regret it. On the eve of the 10th of August he said to the Queen, on seeing her for the last time, "As I am very sure of paying one day with my head for the interest with which your misfortunes have inspired me, I beg of you, Madame, for all recompense, the honor of kissing your hand."

XI.

PÉTION'S ACCOUNT.

IN Barnave we have just seen a man of mind and feeling who, to the ideas and principles of a democrat, united the tact and sense of fitness which are lacking in many a nobleman. One might say that the young deputy from Grenoble was in the royal carriage by way of contrast to Pétion, the other commissioner of the Assembly. The one thought liberalism in nowise incompatible with the tone and manners of good society, while the other fancied that all true demagogues should display a certain rudeness which the vulgar take for austerity. At bottom, Pétion was not a bad man. There was even a sort of sensibility in his soul. But he had heard so many declamations, and he had so often declaimed himself against kings and queens, that the least compassion for them seemed to him a lack of patriotism. He will preserve, then, in the carriage of Louis XVI., the same attitude that he would in the Jacobin club or the club of the Cordeliers. The royal family will see him eat and drink in the berlin in an unmannerly way, throwing his chicken-bones out of the

carriage door at the risk of sending them into
the King's face, and obliging Madame Elisabeth to
pour out his drink without thanking her. It is a
poetic sentiment which animates Barnave's gentle
soul, but the motive power of Pétion's acts and
words is the arrogance of an upstart. A provincial
lawyer, intoxicated with his success in the lower
court of Chartres and his exploits as a lady-killer
in the bourgeois circles of his little town, he did not
doubt that, transplanted to a larger scene, he was
destined to still more brilliant triumphs. Proud of
his position as deputy, and still prouder of his title
and mission as envoy of the Assembly, he felt himself
a sovereign, and delighted in treating Louis XVI. as
his equal, not to say as his inferior. He desired to
teach power a lesson. He spoke *ex cathedra*. He
gave a course in politics. He disputed, he perorated,
he domineered. The account he has left of his journey with the royal family gives the best notion of his
incredible presumption. This document, which was
seized with Pétion's other papers when he fled after
May 31, 1793, is written entirely in his own hand.
M. Mortimer-Ternaux published it for the first time in
his *Histoire de la Terreur*.

The narrative opens magniloquently: "The King's
carriage stops. We go to meet it. An usher pre-
cedes us, and the ceremonial is conducted in an imposing manner. As soon as we are perceived, some
one cries, 'There are the deputies of the National
Assembly!' Everybody hastens to make way for

us. The cortege was superb. There were National
Guards on horseback and on foot, with uniforms and
without them, with arms of all descriptions. The
sun, near its setting, shed its light upon this fair
ensemble in the midst of peaceful fields. I can give
no idea of the sentiment of respect with which we
were surrounded."

Pétion was thirty-two years old. He belonged to
that category of puppies, vain even to artlessness,
who believe themselves irresistible, and imagine that
they produce a profound impression on all women
whatsoever. Lauzun had not more self-confidence
than he. Reader, no matter how prodigious, how
mad, how ridiculous, you may suppose Pétion's fatuity
to have been, it will still surpass your expectation.
He fancied — could you believe it? — that Madame
Elisabeth, Madame Elisabeth herself, the most holy,
the most austere of women, experienced a strong
physical attraction toward him; he thought he saw
in this Princess a Circe, against whom it was necessary for him, for Pétion, if you please, to forearm his
rigid virtue. Listen to him: "Madame Elisabeth
fastened her soft eyes upon me with that air of
languor given by unhappiness, and which inspires a
lively interest. Our glances met several times with
a sort of understanding and attraction. The moon
began to shed her mild radiance. Madame Elisabeth
took Madame Royale upon her knees; afterwards
she placed her half on her own knee and half on
mine. Madame Royale fell asleep. I stretched out

my arm; Madame Elisabeth stretched hers out above
mine. Her glances seemed to me more affecting; I
perceived a certain relaxation of constraint in her
demeanor; her eyes were moist, their melancholy
blended with a sort of sensuous charm. I may
deceive myself, — the sensibility of grief is easily
mistaken for that of pleasure, — but I think that if
we had been alone, that if, as by enchantment, every
one else had vanished, she would have sunk into my
arms."

This supposition flattered the sensual and austere
demagogue, and at the same time it roused his indignation. He adds: "I was so astounded with this
state of affairs that I said to myself: What! can this
be a trick to buy me at such a price? Would Madame
Elisabeth agree to sacrifice her honor in order to
make me lose mine? Yes; nothing costs too much
at court; they are capable of anything. The Queen
could have arranged the plan. And then, considering her unaffected bearing, and self-love also insinu-
ating that she might find me attractive, I became
persuaded, and took pleasure in the thought, that she
was agitated by keen emotions, that she would herself desire that no witnesses were present."

Jean Jacques Rousseau, behold your worthy pupil!
These are the ideas, if not the style and talent, of an
adept of the *Nouvelle Héloïse*. But let pure democrats be reassured. Pétion will not allow himself to
weaken. "I took good care," he says, "not to com-
promise my character. I granted all I could to what

I believed to be Madame Elisabeth's condition; but, nevertheless, without granting enough to permit her to think, or even to suspect, that anything would alter my opinions. I think she understood it wonderfully, and that she saw that the most seductive temptations would be in vain, for I remarked a certain cooling off, a certain severity. which in women often springs from irritated self-love."

The force of truth is such that even from Pétion himself it wrests some just remarks. This enemy of kings and courts, this systematically hostile observer, is astonished to find that something good may be found in royal souls by making diligent search. He recognized in his travelling-companions "an air of simplicity and of family" which pleased him. He deigned to say of Louis XVI.: "Those who do not know the King might be tempted to mistake his timidity for stupidity. But they would be in error. It is very seldom that anything unbecoming escapes him, and I have not heard him make a foolish remark."

Madame Elisabeth inspired him with a sort of involuntary admiration, in spite of the odious and stupid surmises he had just made concerning her. "I should be very much surprised," he says, "if she had not a good and beautiful soul, although one deeply imbued with the prejudices of birth and spoiled by the vices of a court education." There is even a moment when his hatred and inveterate prejudices against Marie Antoinette give place to a less unjust judgment. Inflexible where the Queen is concerned, he becomes almost humane toward the mother. "The Queen," he said, "talked with me about the education of her children. She spoke like the mother of a family and as a sufficiently well-instructed woman. She said that no flattery should be offered to princes, and that it was essential never to tell them anything but the truth." But he quickly repents of his amiability. "I have since learned," he adds, "that this is the fashionable jargon in all the courts of Europe." And he ends by declaring that "the Queen had not, in any sense, either the bearing or the attitude befitting her position."

Marie Antoinette, in her conversation with Pétion, defended her husband's cause energetically. "People blame the King very much," said she; "but they do not really understand the situation in which he is placed. He is constantly told contradictory stories, and he does not know what to believe. Opposing and mutually destructive counsels are given him, one after the other; and he does not know what to do. People complain to him about private misfortunes and murders at the same time. It is all this which determined him to leave the capital. The crown is in suspense over his head. You are not ignorant that there is a party which does not desire a king, and that this party is increasing daily."

Pétion was already republican in theory, but in practice he still remained a royalist. He replied that his principles and sentiments inclined him to prefer

a republican form of government to any other, but
added that there were certain republics which he
would like still less than the despotism of a single
man. Pétion belonged to that class of persons who
like to play with fire, and who say naïvely to the
Revolution, " Thou shalt go no further ! " as if
the Revolution had a mind to listen to them. " It
is not possible," he went on, " to persuade one's self
in good faith that the republican party is to be
dreaded. It is composed of wise and high-principled
men who know how to estimate probabilities, and
who would not risk a general panic which might as
easily lead to despotism as to liberty."

Unhappy Pétion ! How quickly he will descend
the incline which leads to the abyss ! He will be
deadly to the very end, — deadly to the royal family
and to himself ; he is marked with the seal of fatality,
like almost all the actors in the great revolutionary
drama. On the 10th of August in the following
year, he will combine the parts of Judas and Pontius
Pilate. At nightfall he will give Louis XVI. the
kiss of peace, and at daybreak next morning he
will wash his hands of the approaching catastrophe.
He will vote for the King's death, but with a re-
prieve and an appeal to the people, and perhaps this
mitigation of his vote may be caused by the recol-
lection of his journey with the unhappy sovereign.
Condemned himself on May 31, 1793, at the same
time with the Girondins, he will take to flight ; he
will perish miserably in the waste lands near Bor-

deaux, and his body will be found unburied and half devoured by wolves. But we will not anticipate. Let us return to June 23, 1791, and to the road traversed by the royal berlin. It reached Dormans between midnight and one o'clock, June 23–24. "We got out," says Pétion, "at the inn where we had eaten a morsel in coming, and this inn, though passable for a small place, was hardly fit for the reception of the royal family. I confess, however, that I was not sorry to let the court know what an ordinary tavern is like. It was difficult to sleep, because the National Guards and all the people of the neighborhood kept up a constant singing, dancing, and drinking."

They left Dormans June 24, between five and six in the morning. During the day they stopped at Ferté-sous-Jouarre. The mayor of the town, M. Regnard, had sent word that he would be happy to entertain the august travellers, and Louis XVI. accepted the invitation. Here, as at Châlons-sur-Marne, the royal family experienced some consolation. Madame Regnard received them with signs of the most profound respect. "Madame," said Marie Antoinette, accosting her, "you are doubtless the mistress of the house." The mayor's wife returned, with perfect tact, "I was so before Your Majesty entered it." The house was charming, and had a terrace on the shore of the Marne, where Madame Elisabeth chatted with Pétion before dinner. The King himself came out on this terrace to invite the three commissioners of the Assembly to share his repast. All three refused. Madame Regnard and her husband were to pay dear later on for the honor and happiness of having testified their regard for the royal family. On quitting this house, so loyally hospitable, the Queen said to the Dauphin, "My son, thank Madame for her attentions; tell her I shall never forget it." "Mamma thanks you for the care you have taken of us," said the child, "and I love you very much for having given pleasure to mamma."

They set off again at five in the afternoon. The sun was still above the horizon when they arrived before Meaux, that city still so full of souvenirs of the great Bossuet, whose sublime voice alone would have been capable of celebrating the afflictions of the martyr King and Queen. They alighted at the bishop's palace, where they spent the night of June 24-25. After Louis XVI. and Marie Antoinette had taken supper, they had a conversation with Pétion, at the end of which they summoned the three body-guards who had accompanied them ever since they quitted Paris, — MM. de Malden, de Valory, and de Moustier. "At Dormans," the King said to them, "M. Pétion proposed to me to induce you to make your escape, disguised as National Guards. At that time the Queen and I refused, because we thought that it was secretly intended either to assassinate you behind our backs, or to have you arrested and handed over to some military commission; so we said nothing to you about the proposition. But M. Pétion

has just renewed it, and added the barbarous an-
nouncement that at Paris your lives would belong to
the people, so that, since it might be horrible for us
to behold servants whom we appear to love killed
before our eyes, he thought he ought to warn us that
there was not a moment to be lost if escape was to be
attempted. Possibly, in renewing his offer to aid
you, he is acting in better faith than we supposed.
It is for you to determine whether to profit by it."

The three faithful servants fell on their knees
before their kind master. " Sire," cried one of them,
the interpreter of the thoughts of all, " our lives
have been consecrated to Your Majesties. You have
deigned to accept the offering. We know how to
die for you ; it would be a thousand times easier than
to separate from you. Do not doubt, Sire, that death
awaits us, no matter where we turn. Our choice
could not be doubtful. Deign to permit your faithful guards still to accompany you. Grant them to
set off with you to-morrow. May our tears obtain
this last grace." Louis XVI., weeping, granted the
heroic prayer of the three body-guards.

Then the Queen drew her tablets from her pocket
to write down their baptismal names and those of
their fathers, mothers, sisters, and brothers, and also
those of any of their relatives and friends whom, on
her invitation, they dared recommend to Their Majesties. " If we have the grief to lose you," said Marie
Antoinette afterwards, " and if we do not succumb
ourselves beneath the blows of our enemies, be cer-

tain that our benefits will search out your families.
I myself will apprise them of their misfortune, and
at the same time I will let them know the sentiments
toward you which can never leave our hearts."

They left Meaux June 25, at six in the morning.
It was the last day of the fatal journey. "Never,"
says Pétion, "was a day longer and more fatiguing.
The heat was extreme, and we were enveloped in
clouds of dust. The King offered me something to
drink several times, and poured it out himself. We
were twelve whole hours in the carriage without
quitting it for a moment."

A little above Pantin the grenadiers of the National
Guard made their appearance. They disputed with
the cavalry of the escort on the subject of the places
they were to occupy. The grenadiers obliged the
cavalry to fall back, and rough words passed between
them. An affray seemed imminent. Bayonets were
brandished around the carriage, the windows of which
were kept down. According to Pétion there was
reason to fear for the Queen's life. The most ignoble
insults, the most infamous epithets, the entire vocab-
ulary of Billingsgate, were emptied on her. She was
treated as one would not treat a street-walker, a
prostitute. "She need not show us her son," cried
one; "he is not her husband's." The Dauphin,
frightened by the noise and the glitter of the weapons, began to cry with fear. Marie Antoinette, who
was in tears, tried to reassure him. At the same
time, the crowd were furiously demanding the death

of the body-guards. "Down with the yellow coats!" was shouted on all sides. Some proposed tying them to the wheels; others, to cut them in pieces; still others, to burn them alive. The carriage was stopped, and the body-guards were about to perish under the blows of the assassins. The energetic intervention of Barnave saved them. "Drive on," said he to the postilions; "drive on, I tell you! I am in command here." They started on again, the horses going at a foot-pace; the crowd, which constantly increased, became still more hostile. At last they entered Paris. There lay the greatest danger.

XII.

THE RETURN TO THE TUILERIES.

ON this 25th of June, 1791, all Paris is afoot. It is six o'clock in the evening. The berlin containing the royal family arrives at the Barrière de l'Étoile, and goes down the Champs-Élysées to re-enter the Tuileries. Hundreds of thousands of spectators are looking on at the humiliation of royalty. The carriage makes its way slowly between a double row of National Guards. The entry is still more sinister than that of October 6. The monarchy is more vanquished, more cast down. They had set off in the night of Monday and Tuesday, June 20–21. They returned the following Saturday in broad daylight, but this light is more melancholy than that darkness. At the moment of departure, night meant hope. At the hour of return, day meant despair. Ah! that Palace of the Tuileries, how menacing it rises in the distance, with its architecture grandiose and severe! In vain the setting sun illumines it with its ardent flames; it is sombre, forbidding, fatal. In former days the solemn entries into the good city of Paris, the superb capital, were so brilliant, so tri-

umphant! There were such joyous shouts, such acclamations all along the way! The crowd then
regarded the august family with looks of love, tenderness, admiration, and rapture! And Marie Antoinette, happy in being loved, thanked them with such
a charming smile! The soldiers presented arms.
Mothers took their little ones in their arms, and
pointed out to them the King, the Queen, the Dauphin, the young Madame Royale. The drummers
beat the general alarm. The military bands played
Vive Henri IV. The flags were respectfully inclined
before the sovereign. The body-guards with their
brilliant armor, the Swiss in red uniforms, the civil
and military households of the King and Queen, the
Princes and Princesses, the great lords with their blue
ribbons, the great ladies in dazzling toilets and sparkling with precious stones, — all this resplendent
spectacle and pomp of luxury and power ravished a
faithful people and filled them with enthusiasm.

How all is changed to-day! What a doleful scene
is shone on by this sun of June! Scorn in the place of
respect; hatred in the place of love. Truly funereal
procession! Supreme humiliation of the King and
of royalty! Placards have been posted up on which
is written: "Any one who applauds the King will be
beaten; any one who insults him will be hanged."
Such is the change in men's ideas that a proclamation
like this is considered an act of magnanimity.

At first the regulation is obeyed. At the Barrière
de l'Étoile the populace is malicious rather than furi-

ous. Though eyes glow with a savage flame, mouths
are silent. Something like cool indifference modifies
the hatred. But as they draw nearer to the Tuileries,
the order to keep silence is violated. Curses and
insults resound on every side. The heat is oppres-
sive. The clouds of hot dust raised by the tramp of
such a multitude envelops them like a mourning
veil. The royal berlin winds through a forest of
bayonets. Do you see all these faces, made savage
by anger and disdain, — these hats kept on in token
of insolence and rebellion? Do you see the National
Guards reversing their arms as at a funeral? Through
these billows of dust do you see the great captive,
the vanquished man, the King? The King, who like
one accused, — like a criminal, — will be forced humbly to bow his head and implore pardon from his
subjects! Do you recognize the woman who, for her
part, never lowers her head, who is pursued by fate,
who sees misfortune hovering about her like a raven-
ing vulture; but who, amid the most horrible crises
and the most terrifying dangers, never loses that
lofty courage which is her ancestral heritage, and
which is like the very foundation and essence of her
soul?

If Marie Antoinette alone had been in danger, she
would have been as unmoved now in crossing the
Place Louis Quinze as she will be two years later
when she crosses the same accursed spot on her way
to the scaffold. What occupies her is not her own
safety, but that of her husband, her children, her sis-

ter-in-law, and her attendants. For herself, nothing
moves her, nothing makes her turn pale. She soars,
intrepid sovereign that she is, above danger, above
suffering, above death. This cruel throng whose
cries she hears, inspires her not with anger, but with
pity. If she does not remain absolutely unmoved, it
is because she is thinking about her children. The
Dauphin's forehead is dripping with sweat. He can
hardly breathe. "See, gentlemen," says the unhappy
mother to the National Guards, who march on either
side the carriage, "see what a state my poor children are in; they are choking." "We will choke
you in another fashion!" mutters an infamous voice.

The carriages arrive at the revolving bridge at the
end of the Place Louis Quinze, opposite the Tuileries.
It is closed as soon as they cross it. But the garden
is packed with an innumerable crowd. The danger
increases as they come nearer to the palace. It is
a question whether they will reach it safe and sound,
and the same emotions are caused by the thought of
re-entrance as had been by that of going away. Anguish at the departure, anguish at the return. The
greatest perils are incurred by the three body-guards,
who have remained on the box of the royal berlin.
The exasperated crowd clamor loudly for their death.
Is the blood of these faithful companions of the fatal
journey to spurt out on the Queen's robe? Are these
three devoted servants to be the victims cast to the
tigerish rabble? The carriages which have slowly
and with difficulty opened their way, arrive at last

before the three steps of the terrace which separates
the palace from the garden. At once the assassins
spring towards the three body-guards, anxious to
seize their prey. The royal family are requested to
alight at once so as to avoid the sight of the murders
about to be committed. But in spite of the danger
they incur themselves, they will not stir, hoping that
their presence may save their wretched servants.
The murderers, in redoubled rage, begin to scramble
up to the coachman's box, where MM. de Moustier,
de Malden, and de Valory still remain. Fearing lest
the prolongation of the struggle may imperil the lives
of the King and his family, the three victims resolve
to end it by voluntarily coming down and delivering
themselves to the assassins.

Madame Elisabeth, perceiving this movement,
passes her arm through a window in the front of
the berlin and seizes the skirt of M. de Valory's
waistcoat, to prevent him from jumping down. But
he and his comrades reach the ground, and offering themselves as holocausts to the crowd, advance
heroically into the midst of their murderers. They
are seized and thrown down, dragged about by the
hair, and covered with blows. Fortunately, some
honest National Guards intervene, and, wresting the
three body-guards from the savages, conduct them,
but not without great difficulty, into the palace.

The royal family then leave the carriage. The
distance is short between the three steps of the terrace where the carriage had stopped and the door

of the Pavilion of the Horloge. But the terrace,
like the garden, is thronged by an immense crowd,
whose manner is so threatening, especially toward the
Queen, that the passage, short though it be, is dangerous enough. The King is the first one to alight.
The people are silent, but keep their hats on. Only
one man, M. de Guilhermy, a member of the National
Assembly, uncovers respectfully. " Put your hat on
again ! " is shouted from all sides. But he throws it
into the midst of the crowd, too far to be brought
back to him, and cool and fearless, remains respectful
amidst universal insult, his face calm and his head
bare.

Marie Antoinette next leaves the carriage. At
sight of her, hostile mutterings become audible.
During all this time the National Assembly is in
session close to the Tuileries. It does not choose to
interrupt its business on account of a king. A king
is such a small affair nowadays. Still, a few deputies,
some through respect, and others through curiosity,
have come to the terrace to witness the arrival of
the royal family. Among them is one who favors
the new ideas, the Vicomte de Noailles. He hastens
to approach the Queen and offer her his arm. Marie
Antoinette refuses the protection of an adversary,
and asks that of a deputy of the right, whom she
has just recognized. " The dignity of the empire,"
as M. de Lamartine has said, " is found entire in the
gesture and the heart of a woman."

One of the officers of the King's bedchamber, M.

Hue, manages to reach the carriage, and holds out his arms to receive his master's son. The eyes of the little Prince fill with tears on perceiving this faithful servant. But in spite of all M. Hue's efforts to seize the Dauphin, an officer of the National Guard takes possession of the child, carries him quickly into the palace, and sets him down on the table in the council hall of the Ministers.

Separated from her son, Marie Antoinette has a moment of great anxiety concerning the child's fate. She enters the palace with the King, Madame Elisabeth, and Madame Royale. Oh! what a doleful re-entrance. Never has a dungeon seemed more fatal to prisoners. No; this is no longer a palace, it is the vestibule of the scaffold. One might say the royal family passed under the Caudine Forks in entering the Pavilion of the Horloge. They ascend the great staircase to the first story. Before reaching their apartments they cross the hall, where the three body-guards are already prisoners, and make signs testifying their emotion and their joy at seeing them still alive. M. de Malden had received several bayonet thrusts. M. de Moustier had been struck in the neck with the blade of an axe. M. de Valory, knocked down with the butt end of a musket and dragged around by his hair, had been extremely bruised. They were rejoiced to have suffered for their King and Queen. "What masters!" exclaimed M. de Valory in his narrative, "and how well they merited that one should die for them!"

At last, behold Louis XVI. once more within the
palace of his fathers. He reappears there a vanquished man, whose crown is no longer anything
but a derisive bauble. This is not a real monarch;
it is only the phantom of a king. And yet the force
of habit is such that the old etiquette machine works
still, as if its momentum were not quite exhausted.
Louis XVI. finds himself in his apartments as if
nothing had happened since the beginning of the
week. He is served as usual; it seems as though
he might have just returned from a hunting excursion.
The reception in his bedchamber will take place with
all customary ceremony.

Camille Desmoulins, in Number 83 of his journal,
the *Révolutions de France et de Brabant,* thus attempted to cast ridicule upon the King's return to
the Tuileries: "When Louis XVI. re-entered his
apartment, he threw himself into an armchair, saying, 'It is devilish hot.' Then, 'I made a wretched
journey there. But it had been running in my head
this long time.' Afterwards, looking at the National
Guards, who were present, 'It was a foolish thing I
did; I grant it. But why shouldn't I play tricks as
well as any one else? Let some one bring me a
chicken!' One of his valets-de-chambre came in.
'Ah! you're there, are you? And I too, I'm here!'
The chicken was brought. Louis XVI. ate and
drank with an appetite that would have done honor
to the King of Cocagne."

In Number 84 of his journal, Camille Desmoulins

complained that the National Assembly treated the
King, now become a prisoner, altogether too well.
"It will not do to dance attendance," he said, "to
suffer a criminal to get into a bath on the arrival of
the commissioners. It will not do to wait until he is
in his bath-tub, and rings a bell to admit the National
Assembly like a bath-waiter. Did any one ever hear
of judges writing down their names, and sending
them up by a prison porter, to ask humbly for an
interview with a criminal, and his hour for being
interrogated? Never was there such a contemptible
action."

If anger and irony like this is what the revolutionists feel, the royalists experience profound sadness and compassion. In order to get an idea of it,
read this passage from the Memoirs of the Marquis
de Ferrières, describing a scene that took place as
Louis XVI. was re-entering his capital in humiliation: "An old military man, a chevalier of Saint
Louis, was wandering from one place to another, the
prey of a most tormenting anxiety. Reaching a
retired spot, he was surprised to see one of the
Parisian horse-guards, who was weeping. The old
military man approached him. 'Comrade,' said he,
'who could have distressed you to such a point as
this?' 'Ah! sir,' answered the horse-guard, sobbing,
'I have abandoned my post; I could not keep it.
The sight I have just seen has tortured my heart.
And I am not the only one; for my poor horse,
which I took back to the stable, will not eat.' The

old military man, with tears in his eyes, rummaged in
his pocket. ' My friend, I have only these eighteen
francs; do me the favor to accept them.' The horse-
guard repelled them with his hand, crying sorrow-
fully, 'Ah! I see very well that no one believes
any longer in a soldier's honor!' The old soldier
threw himself into the arms of this worthy man.
Both of them, in expressive silence, mingled in this
embrace their profound despair and the lively mutual
esteem they had conceived for each other." Does
not this naïve anecdote recall the legends of the
Middle Ages?

The Assembly had passed that morning a decree,
the first article of which runs thus: " As soon as the
King shall arrive at the Palace of the Tuileries, a
guard shall be provisionally assigned him, which,
under the orders of the commandant general of the
Parisian guard, shall secure his safety and be answerable for his person." Other articles had decreed a
similar guard for the heir-presumptive, and one for
the Queen. Moreover, the Assembly ordained that
all those who had accompanied the royal family in
their flight should be put under arrest, and interrogated. The King was provisionally suspended from
the functions of royalty, and the Minister of the
Interior was ordered to proclaim the decree instantly,
by sound of trumpet, in every quarter of the capital.

Night has come. The fugitives are under a sort
of hallucination. Their ears are still deafened with
the incessant clamor of the last four days. Worn

out by fatigue and emotions of every kind, they are
going to seek repose. But the rest they will take is
a rest full of anguish. If he is still living as a man,
Louis XVI. is dead as a king. They promise him
that he shall rise again. But at what price, and
what manner of precarious life will it be which they
throw him as a bounty after galvanizing his royal
power? He no longer dares either to act or speak.
He hardly dares to breathe. If he sighs, it is
reckoned to him as a crime. A tear would be his
condemnation. Day and night he must listen without complaining to the obscene and cruel talk that
goes on beneath his windows. The garden of the
Tuileries is now only a revolutionary camp, where
the hawkers of journals and pamphlets cry their
wares, where conspirators plot, and the regicidal
knife is slowly sharpened. That beautiful garden,
the former meeting-place of elegance and fashion,
is as much an arena of anarchy and disorder as that
of the Palais Royal. Just beside it, on the site of the
future rue de Rivoli and rue de Castiglione, is the
Hall of the Manège, where the National Assembly,
the inheritor of the rights of the crown, holds its sessions as sovereign. It is in the narrow space between
the Place du Carrousel and the Hall of the Manège
that royalty writhes and agonizes painfully. The
palace and the garden, the lanes which bound them
on the west, the place which bounds them on the
east, all are fatal, all breathe discord and rebellion.
One might say that threatening voices sound from

every stone and tree. There is something deadly in the atmosphere. Catherine de' Medici was right in dreading the Tuileries as a residence foredoomed to calamities. In this palace, or better, in this prison, the heir of Saint Louis, of Henri IV., and Louis XIV. is no longer a king: he is a hostage.

THIRD PART.

THE CLOSE OF 1791.

I.

THE CAPTIVITY IN THE TUILERIES.

THE next morning after the return from Varennes, June 26, 1791, the Dauphin said on waking: "I had a frightful dream. I was surrounded by wolves and tigers and savage beasts that wanted to eat me up." It was not the child only, but the whole royal family, which had been violently disturbed by the shock of the fatal journey. They awoke captives in the Tuileries. They could form no illusions on that head. The palace was a prison. Wishing to assure himself if he were really a captive, the King presented himself at a door where a sentry was on guard.

"Do you recognize me?" asked Louis XVI.

"Yes, Sire," replied the sentry.

And the King was obliged to go back.

The master of the Tuileries was no longer the sovereign, but M. de Gouvion, the major-general of the National Guard and the executor of M. de Lafayette's commands. He had asked for and obtained the right to take whatever precautions he deemed necessary, and notably that of walling up several doors in the interior of the palace. No one could enter it without a card of admission obtained from him. Even those engaged in the domestic service of the royal family were searched on going out and coming in. Madame Elisabeth wrote to Madame de Bombelles, July 10: "They have established a sort of camp beneath the windows of the King and Queen, lest they should jump down into the garden, which is hermetically sealed and filled with soldiers." A real camp was, indeed, to be seen there, with tents and all else necessary to the installation of troops. Sentries were posted everywhere, even on the roofs.

The Queen's women found the greatest difficulty in getting access to her apartments. It had been resolved that she should have no personal attendant except the lady's-maid who had acted as a spy before the journey to Varennes. A portrait of this person was placed at the foot of the staircase leading to the Queen's rooms, so that the sentinel should permit no other woman to enter. Louis XVI. was obliged to appeal to Lafayette in order to have this spy turned out of the palace, where her presence was an outrage on Marie Antoinette.

This espionage and inquisition pursued the unfortunate Queen even into her bedroom. The guards

were instructed not to lose sight of her by night or
day. They took note of her slightest gestures, listened to her slightest words. Stationed in the room
adjoining hers, they kept the communicating door
always open, so that they could see the august captive at all times. One day, Louis XVI. having closed
this door, the officer on guard reopened it. "Those
are my orders," said he. "I will open it every time.
If Your Majesty closes it, Your Majesty will give
yourself a useless trouble."

Marie Antoinette caused the bed of her lady's-
maid to be placed close to hers, so that, as it could
be rolled about and was provided with curtains, it
might prevent her being seen by the officers. One
night, while the maid was sleeping profoundly, and
the Queen sitting up, the officer entered the bedchamber to give some political advice to his sovereign. Marie Antoinette told him to speak low, so
as not to disturb the sleeping woman. She awoke,
however, and was seized with mortal terror at seeing
an officer of the National Guard so near the Queen.
"Be calm," Marie Antoinette said to her, "and do
not rise. The person whom you see is a good French-
man, deceived concerning the intentions and position
of his sovereign, but whose language shows that he
has a real attachment to the King."

When the Queen went up to see the Dauphin, by
the inner staircase which connected the ground-floor
on which her apartment was situated with the first
floor where her children and her husband slept, she

invariably found his door locked. One of the officers of the National Guard knocked at it, saying, "The Queen!" At this signal, the two officers who kept watch over the governess of the children of France opened the door.

It was the height of summer. If, towards evening, the King and his family wanted a breath of fresh air, they could not show themselves at the windows of their palace without being exposed to the insults and invectives of the people who were on the terrace.

Every day, deputations from different quarters of the city, suspicious and determined to see for themselves what precautions were taken and what vigilance exercised, would arrive at the Tuileries. At night the King and Queen would be awakened to make sure they had not taken flight. M. de Lafayette or M. de Gouvion were roused up also, to warn them of pretended attempts to escape. The alarms were continual. August 25, Madame Elisabeth wrote: "To-night a sentinel who was in a corridor up stairs fell asleep, dreamed I don't know what, and woke up screaming. In an instant, every guard, as far as the end of the Louvre gallery, did the same. In the garden, also, there was a terrible panic."

The precautions taken were so rigorous, that it was forbidden to say Mass in the palace chapel, because the distance between it and the apartments of Louis XVI. and Marie Antoinette was thought too great. A corner of the Gallery of Diana, where a wooden altar was erected, bearing an ebony crucifix and a few vases of flowers, became the only spot where the son of Saint Louis, the Most Christian King, could hear Mass.

And yet, among the guards, now transformed into veritable jailers, there were to be found some well intentioned men who testified a respectful regard for the royal family, and sought to lessen the severity of the orders they had received. Such was Saint Prix, an actor at the Comédie-Française. A sentinel was always on duty in the dark and narrow corridor behind the Queen's apartments which divided the ground-floor in two. The post was not in great demand, and Saint Prix often asked for it. He facilitated the short interviews which the King and Queen had in this corridor, and if he heard the slightest noise, he gave them warning. Marie Antoinette had reason, also, to praise M. Collot, chief of battalion of the National Guard, who was charged with the military service of her apartment. One day an officer on duty there spoke unjustly of the Queen. M. Collot wished to inform M. de Lafayette and have him punished; but Marie Antoinette opposed this with her usual kindliness, and said a few judicious and good-tempered words to the culprit. He was converted in an instant, and became one of her most devoted partisans.

The royal family endured their captivity with admirable sweetness and resignation, and concerned themselves less about their own fate than that of the persons compromised by the Varennes journey, who

were now incarcerated. Louis XVI., instead of in-
dulging in recriminations against men and things,
offered his humiliations and sufferings to God. He
prayed, he read, he meditated. Next to his prayer-
book his favorite reading was the life of Charles I.,
either because he sought, in studying history, to find
a way of escaping an end like that of the unfortunate
monarch, or because an analogy of sorrows and disasters had established a profound and mysterious sympathy between the king who had been beheaded and
the king who was soon to be so.

The sister of Louis XVI. was like a good angel
near him. Gentler, more pious, more resigned than
ever, she possessed that supreme energy which comes
from a good conscience and a fearless heart. July 4,
she wrote to the Count de Provence, the future
Louis XVIII., who, having taken refuge abroad, was
out of danger: " Heaven had its own designs in pre-
serving you. God at least wills your salvation. That
is what I most desire. You know whether my heart
is sincere when it wishes for your eternal welfare
before all things else. We are well, and we love
you; but I count myself chief in that respect. . . .
Never think lightly of those whom the hand of God
has stricken hard, but to whom He will give, I hope,
the means to endure the trial. I embrace you with
all my heart."

July 23, Madame Elisabeth wrote to Madame de
Raigecourt: "I am still a little stunned by the violent shock we have experienced. I should need a

few tranquil days, far away from the bustle of Paris, to restore me to myself. But as God does not permit that, I hope He will make it up to me in some other way. Ah, my heart! happy is the man who, holding his soul always in his hands, sees nothing but God and eternity, and has no other aim than to make the evils of this world conduce to the glory of God, and to profit by them, in order to enjoy in peace an eternal recompense."

It was in religion that the saintly Princess ever found strength, hope, and consolation. "You cannot imagine," she wrote to the Abbé de Lubersac, July 29, "how fervent souls redouble their zeal. Perhaps Heaven will not be deaf to so many prayers, offered with so much confidence. It is from the heart of Jesus that they seem to expect the grace that is needed. The fervor of this devotion seems redoubled." Madame Elisabeth, although not renouncing hope, probably comprehended better than any one the extreme gravity of the situation. She had written to Madame de Bombelles the day before : "I dread the moment when the King will be in a position to act. There is not a single intelligent man here in whom we can have confidence. You know where that will lead us ; I shudder at it. We must lift our hands to heaven ; God will have pity on us. Ah, how I wish that others beside ourselves would join in the prayers which are addressed Him by all the religious communities and all the pious souls of France ! "

The sentiments of the Queen were neither less

touching nor less lofty than those of her sister-in-law. Marie Antoinette devoted a part of every day to the education of her children and that of an orphan named Ernestine Lambriquet, whose mother had been one of Madame Royale's servants. The hapless sovereign adduced herself as an example of the instability of worldly grandeur. She taught her pupils to deprive themselves voluntarily, every month, of part of the money intended for their pleasures, in order to give it to the poor; and the children, worthy of their mother, considered this privation as a happiness. Marie Antoinette bore her griefs with a courage which was all the more meritorious, because the emotions of the fatal Varennes journey had made her suffer immensely in body, and still more in mind. Madame Campan, who had been away from her several weeks, and returned in August, describes her thus: " I found her getting out of bed. Her countenance was not extremely altered; but after the first kind words she addressed to me, she took off her cap, and told me to see what effect grief had produced on her hair. In a single night it had become as white as that of a woman of seventy. Her Majesty showed me a ring which she had just had made for the Princess de Lamballe. It was a sheaf of her white hair, with this inscription: ' Whitened by misfortune.' "

Alas! the Queen of France and Navarre is no longer the dazzling sovereign who triumphed like a goddess. She is no longer the radiant Juno of the royal Olympus, the superb beauty whose charm is equalled only by her prestige. She is no longer followed by a train of adorers, who fall into raptures as she passes by. No one celebrates the splendor of her royal person, the luxury of her toilets, the sparkle of her jewels and her diadem. No. But in this palace which is now only a prison, in this captivity full of anguish and of tears, there is something venerable, august, sacred; something which is graver, more imposing, and more majestic than supreme power: it is sorrow. Ah! now is the moment when souls truly chivalrous can and ought to devote themselves to this woman. This is the hour when her courtiers honor themselves more than they honor her. O Queen! you are persecuted. For you the *Hosannas* are changed into *Crucificatur!* Under the very windows of your palace you are calumniated, threatened, insulted. Hither, then, ye courtiers of misfortune! Hasten, one and all! Here your zeal will be well placed. Here no one comes to seek favors, money, earthly goods. Here there is peril, sacrifice, and death. Come! the Queen will honor you. She will write your name in the golden book of the faithful. Come! the cloud which overshadows her beautiful forehead renders it still more noble. Her glances are less animated than of old, but they are more affecting. There is something austere and melancholy in her whole aspect now, which even the most ardent revolutionists cannot contemplate too closely without profound and inexpressible emotion. Come all! and if you feel no pity for the Queen, you will bend before the woman, before the wife, before the mother.

II.

UNTIL further orders, Louis XVI. is a dispossessed sovereign. During this interregnum Paris presents all manner of contrasts. It is a medley of optimism and sinister previsions, of monarchical relics and republican germs. According to some, all evil is at an end and good has begun; the age of gold is following the age of iron; order and liberty are united forever. According to others, a series of terrific tempests is setting in. Behold! say they, what black clouds hang on the horizon: riot, revolution, famine, religious war, civil war, foreign war, invasion, dismemberment, calamities of every kind. Meanwhile there is contention everywhere. On this side the Jacobins, more revolutionary than the Revolution itself; on that, the conservatives, more royalist than the King. Lack of discipline in the army; schism in religion; in the salons, no less than in the public resorts, quarrelling, hatred, invective. At the theatres every play gives rise to allusions and conflicts: at the Français the Saint Bartholomew scenes of Joseph Chénier's *Charles IX.*

carry public fury even to convulsions; at the Opera,
the royalists enthusiastically applaud, while the republicans hiss with rage, this line from *Castor et
Pollux :* —

" Reign over a faithful people ";

at the Nation, *Athalie* with Gossec's choruses, the
partisans of throne and altar growing ecstatic over
the monarchical passages of Racine's masterpiece, and
the revolutionists applying to Marie Antoinette the
anathemas against the daughter of Jezebel. In every
street and square are gatherings, seditious propositions,
public criers, who hawk about calumny and lies; in
the galleries of the Palais Royal, the abode of anarchy
and debauch, the ever-increasing and impure stream
of ruffians and prostitutes; in the journals a torrent
of diatribes, an avalanche of false news, a deluge of
infamies. It is Camille Desmoulins who says: " Nowadays, journalists exercise the public ministry. They
denounce, decree, absolve, or condemn daily ; they
ascend the orator's tribune, and there are stentorian
lungs among them which make themselves heard
by the eighty-three departments. The journals rain
every morning like manna from heaven, and fifty
sheets come like the sun every day to light up the
horizon."

The press is furious, insane. In order to get
readers it must dip its pen in vitriol and filth, before
dipping it in blood. Wisdom, decorum, moderation,
what chimeras are those ! We are not in the Acad-

cmy. We are in the fish-market, at the cross-roads, in the kennels. What pleases is obscene language, the ribaldry of clowns at the fair, mean and cruel jests, and the savage cries of cannibals. Violence, rage, and frenzy are the fashion. Carra, in the *Annales patriotiques;* Fréron, in the *Orateur du peuple;* Camille Desmoulins, in the *Révolutions de France et de Brabant;* Condorcet, in the *Chronique de Paris;* Fauchet, in the *Bouche de fer;* Marat, in the *Ami du peuple;* Brissot, in the *Patriote français;* Laclos, author of the *Liaisons dangereuses,* in the *Journal des Jacobins,* contend with each other which shall bawl longest and loudest. What agitations, what follies, what unhealthy ambitions, what ridiculous vanities, what stupid or criminal chimeras there are in this ant-hill, which sooner or later the heel of a despot will trample down.

Lafayette is no better treated than Louis XVI. Camille Desmoulins thus apostrophizes the famous general: "Liberator of two worlds, flower of janizaries, phœnix of chief-constables, Don Quixote of Capet and the two Chambers, constellation of the white horse, my voice is too feeble to rise above the clamor of your thirty thousand spies and the noise of your four hundred drums." The same journalist calls the King, "Our crowned Sancho Panza." Paid colporteurs distributed in public places the pamphlet entitled: *Grand jugement rendu par le peuple contre Louis XVI.* "O day of triumph!" is said in it, "O Frenchmen, how happy you are! The perjurer is arrested. Frenchmen, this fall should be an example to you. The traitor Louis should suffer his punishment." The *Bouche de fer* thus expresses itself: " There is no room for deliberation ; the free people, the sovereign people, have put their hats on while looking contemptuously at the *ci-devant* King. Behold at last a plébiscite ; the Republic is sanctioned."

Every possible means of making the King odious and ridiculous is sought for. He is represented in caricatures with the body of a swine and the forehead of a ram. If the Orleanists and republicans are to be believed, he has lost his reason. He demands post-horses, he wants to put himself at the head of his troops and fight his enemies ; at another moment he proposes to abdicate ; the next instant he gets into a rage, seizes stools and throws at the mirrors in his apartment, and breaks the china vases. These stupid fables are repeated all over Paris. The people have lost completely all sentiment of respect.

Even the churches are no longer places of consolation. There is discord there as elsewhere. In the eyes of the faithful, the constitutional priests who officiate are apostates and intruders. Each religious ceremony celebrated by them is a profanation, a sacrilege. The Pope has struck the ecclesiastical rebels with his thunderbolts. It is the abomination of desolation. The pious people who still enter the churches, shudder there with grief and sacred anger.

At the National Assembly the discussions become more and more tumultuous. Republican sentiment

no longer hides itself; Robespierre is the idol of the
day. "That man bears me great ill will," says Louis
XVI.; "for me, I bear him none; for I do not know
him." The party of order might confide in Barnave,
Duport, and Malouet, and with their aid modify the
Constitution on monarchical principles. But the
members of the Right are not willing to do this. In
their view, to recognize the Constitution, even by
correcting it, would be to sanction revolt. To join
hands with the seditious would be to become seditious
themselves. " Our hopes," say they, " have not fallen
so low that we see nothing left but to accept a part
in a comedy of frightened revolutionists. No con-
cessions, no transactions. Good will spring from the
excess of evil. The trial must be made, and made
thoroughly, so that the democrats may display the
full extent of their rascality and folly!" Developing
this thesis, which is the excuse alleged by all compromised causes when it is sought to justify their
inaction and their decay, the royalists systematically
abstain from voting; they sulk, they give a paltry,
impotent, and peevish character to their opposition.

Paris has become a pandemonium. What moder-
ate man could make himself heard in the midst of
such a howling storm? It would need the trump of
the last judgment to drown this noise, to dominate
this tumult. Who, then, could have the audacity to
seize the helm? Who would have sufficient moral
and material force to inspire the passengers with confidence and restore discipline among the mutinous

crew? There is no pilot. The vessel is about to go to pieces on the reefs. The sky is furrowed with lightning.

The month of July, 1791, did not fail to please people thirsting after spectacles and emotions: the 12th, the removal of Voltaire's remains; the 14th, the Fête of the Federation in the Champ-de-Mars; the 17th, a riot where blood flowed in torrents: certainly a well-filled month!

Rejoice, free-thinkers! Behold the triumph of philosophy, the apotheosis of your patriarch of Ferney! When he died, his body was taken by his nephew, furtively and by night, to the church of the Abbey of Sellières, in Champagne. But now the city of Paris desires that the illustrious dead shall be placed in the Panthéon, that cathedral of philosophers. The revolutionists burn incense to Voltaire, who was the sworn enemy of the Revolution; to Voltaire, the guest of all great nobles, the courtier of all kings. The procession starts from the Place de la Bastille. The coffin is raised up so that the crowd can see it, and the pedestal for it is built of stones torn from the foundations of the fortress of the old régime. On one of the stones the following inscription was engraved: "Receive, in this place whither thou wert dragged by despotism, the honors thy country decrees to thee."

Forty market porters, vested in white albs, their arms bare, and their heads crowned with laurels, represent the ancient poets, and carry on a stretcher a statue of the demigod in gilt pasteboard. A golden casket in the form of an ark contains the seventy volumes of his works. The coffin is placed on a car drawn by twelve white horses, whose manes and bridle reins are braided with flowers. Porters costumed as priests of Apollo, and harlots in more or less dingy robes, figuring as nymphs and muses, surround the car. All the actors and actresses of Paris walk behind it. It halts before the principal theatres and the house of M. de Villette, where Voltaire died, and where his heart is preserved. Wreaths and garlands ornament the façade on which is the inscription: " His mind is everywhere, and his heart is here."

The Théâtre Français has converted its peristyle into a triumphal arch. A statue of the author of *Mérope* is erected there. On its pedestal one reads: " He wrote *Irène* when he was eighty-three; at seventeen he wrote *Œdipe*." Notwithstanding the eagerness of the crowd, this mythological and pagan pomp, this funeral ceremony without a cross, without priests, and without prayers, excited nothing but curiosity. These strange white-robed priestesses, these would-be vestals, whose mission it is to keep alive the sacred fire of poesy, create a smile. It is not an easy thing to accord to a man, without becoming ridiculous, the honors due to God alone. Do what you can, say what you will, the Voltaire cult will never be a religion.

A pouring rain suddenly disturbs the procession.

Poets, muses, nymphs, municipal officers, all run to seek a shelter. The ceremony is not over until half-past ten at night. The body is deposited in the Panthéon between those of Descartes and Mirabeau. The royalists complain because a public fête has been celebrated while the King and his family are captives in the Tuileries. Charitable persons regret the sums expended on a theatrical display while the people lack bread. All those who figured in the procession are tired out and covered with mud. The rain has chilled enthusiasm. The gilt pasteboard of the statue is soaked into fragments. To-morrow no one will give another thought to the patriarch of Ferney. *Sic transit gloria mundi!*

Two days after the translation of Voltaire's remains comes the Fête of the Federation in the Champ-de-Mars. The sequestrated royal family is not present. The optimism and the illusions of the preceding year are already long gone by. People perceive that the age of gold is not quite so near as they supposed. The acclamations are less enthusiastic; the blare of the trumpets wakes different echoes.

The epilogue of the fête of July 14 is the bloody scene of July 17. Men's minds are too excited. An address to Frenchmen, signed by Achille du Châtelet, afterwards colonel of a regiment of chasseurs, had been placarded on all the walls of Paris, and even in the corridors of the National Assembly. "Citizens," it is said in this address, "the perfect tranquillity, the mutual confidence which reigned

among us during the flight of the *ci-devant* King,
and the profound indifference with which we saw
him brought back, are unequivocal signs that the
absence of a king is better than his presence, and
that he is not merely a superfluity, but an over-
heavy burden which weighs down the whole nation.
The history of France presents nothing but a long
succession of the sufferings of the people, the cause
of which may always be traced back to the Kings.
We have not ceased to suffer for them and by them.
The catalogue of their oppressions was full. But
to their crimes treason alone was lacking. To-day
nothing is lacking; the measure is complete; there
is no crime remaining to be committed. Their reign
is ended. . . . As to the individual safety of M.
Louis Bourbon, it is all the more assured, seeing that
France will not dishonor itself by resentment against
a man who has accomplished his own dishonor."

The Orleanists and the Jacobins unite. In a petition in which it is declared that "it is as contrary to
the majesty of the outraged nation as it is to its interests, ever again to confide the reins of empire to a
perjured, traitorous, and fugitive man." Brissot and
Laclos demand another king. The petition is posted
on all the walls. Public notification is given that all
those who wish to sign the original go to the Champ-
de-Mars, where it lies on the Altar of the Country,
left standing since the Fête of the 14th. Sunday,
July 17, is fixed for these signatures. The advocates
of the deposition arrive in crowds at the Champ-de-

Mars at three in the afternoon; but Lafayette and
Bailly oppose the manifestation. The municipality
has decided to display the red flag and proclaim mar-
tial law. The rioters shout: "Down with the red
flag! down with the bayonets!" A hail of stones
follows these vociferations. The National Guards
fire several times in the air. Some of the people take
to flight. But the leaders, recovering from their
first fright, on seeing that no one is wounded rally
the flying. They begin to throw stones again. Lafayette orders a second discharge, which this time
is real. The ground is covered with dead bodies.
From the Champ-de-Mars the panic spreads in every
direction. Parisians who are taking the air in the
Champs Élysées are appalled. If Lafayette chose, it
would be all up with republican outbreaks for a long
time. The demagogues think they are lost. They
tremble. But the next day they are permitted to raise
their heads; their journals reappear. They return
tranquilly to their clubs. Reassured by the hesitation
of their adversaries, they requite it by audacity, and
the Revolution goes on its way.

There are many who are deeply afflicted by these
scandals and troubles. But the greater number find
a sort of pleasure in them. This perpetual agitation,
this political fury, these violent emotions, these
shocks, these unforeseen and rapid crises which succeed each other like so many scenes in a melodrama,
please many persons greatly. They have become so
accustomed to fever that they do not desire health.

Repose would weary minds so eager after exciting scenes. They are interested in parliamentary contentions as Spaniards are in bull fights. It is the same effervescence, the same shouts, the same tumult. It is all the more agreeable to them to see the giants falling, because, in former days, they could only be looked at kneeling. The instinct of equality finds satisfaction in the levelling of the throne. The sufferings of royalty, of the clergy, and of the nobility are the delights of the common people. Honest citizens and National Guards rejoice in the lessons administered to power, and the future Septembrists already scent an odor of blood in the air.

III.

THE EMIGRATION.

W E have just looked at Paris. Now let us cast a rapid glance at foreign parts.

The tidings of the flight of the King and his family had awakened delirious joy abroad. The émigrés began to entertain the most flattering hopes. They felicitated, they embraced each other. At Brussels great entertainments were preparing in expectation of the courier who should announce that Louis XVI. had happily crossed the frontier. The disaster at Varennes came to chill this overflow of joy.

The emigration which, thus far, had not been very extensive, now became almost general among the nobility, the clergy, and even the upper middle class. In Paris and the chief provincial cities, committees were appointed to facilitate this universal flight. Wild enthusiasts urged the nobles to abandon their families and their estates, and fly like exiles to a foreign country. It was a grand mistake; the place for the nobility was beside the King, not elsewhere. That a loyal aristocracy should follow an exiled sovereign is comprehensible; but that it should

242

abandon him to the gravest perils in his own dominions, and go wandering from court to court instead of remaining where it belongs and playing a national part, seems inadmissible. If the émigrés had employed at home half the energy and the efforts which they fruitlessly employed abroad, the throne would have been saved. But passion does not reason. It is only a question of a little trip to the borders of the Rhine, said they. In five or six weeks we shall come back triumphant. All one has to do is to show his crest, a white handkerchief, the Prince of Condé's boot, and six francs' worth of cord to hang the revolutionary chiefs with.

Exasperated by the failure of the Varennes journey, the Marquis de Bouillé anathematized the National Assembly. A new Coriolanus, he threatened his country with the thunderbolts of his wrath and vengeance. He wrote a letter from Luxembourg to the Assembly. "The King," he says in it, "has just made an effort to break the chains in which you have so long detained him and his unfortunate family. But a blind destiny which governs empires, and against which human prudence avails nothing, has determined otherwise. He is still your prisoner. His life and that of his Queen are — I shudder at the thought — at the mercy of a people whom you have rendered ferocious and sanguinary, and who have become an object of scorn to the universe." The irascible general thus accentuates his threat: "I know better than any one what means of defence you have at command; they amount to nothing. Your chastisement will serve as an example to posterity. . . . You will answer for the safety of the King and his family, I do not say to me, but to all kings, and I declare to you, that if a single hair of his head is touched, not one stone of Paris will be left upon another. I know the roads; I will drive invading armies through them. This letter is but the herald of the manifesto of all European sovereigns. They will teach you, in more emphatic style, what you have to do and what you have to fear. Adieu, gentlemen; I end without compliments. My sentiments are known to you."

During this time the King's two brothers, the future Louis XVIII. and the future Charles X., were seeking to form a European coalition against the Revolution. Their uncle Louis Wenceslas, Elector of Trèves, had received them at Coblentz with cordial hospitality. Coblentz was at this time the Paris of Germany. The head of the house of Condé organized there the staffs of the Princes' army; plenty of officers, no soldiers; a head, but a head separated from the trunk. Calonne had the administration of finances, which was very like a sinecure. Marshal de Broglie was Minister of War. They allotted all the offices of State in advance, as Pompey's Roman knights did on the eve of Pharsalia.

The hero of the emigration was the King of Sweden, whose portrait has been so well drawn by M. Geffroy in his admirable work, *Gustave III. et la cour de France.* On his arrival at Aix-la-Chapelle, Gustavus did not wholly share the illusions of the French émigrés. June 16, 1791, he wrote: "I have found here nearly all the chief nobility of France. These illustrious exiles form a very agreeable society. They are all animated with equal hatred against the National Assembly, and have, besides, such exaggerated notions on all subjects as you can form no idea of. It is really both sad and curious to listen to and observe them." But the Swedish monarch soon felt the influence of his environment. The imprisonment of Louis XVI. in the Tuileries made him indignant.

Very proud of the golden sword Marie Antoinette had sent him, with this device, *For the defence of the oppressed*, the King of Sweden held court at Aix-la-Chapelle, with Fersen, d'Escar, Breteuil, Calonne, M. and Madame de Saint Priest, the Marquis de Bouillé, and Mesdames d'Harcourt, de Croy, and de Lamballe.

Of a bold and chivalrous spirit, fond of adventure, and burning with the desire to attract public attention and make himself talked about by kings and peoples, Gustavus became intoxicated with the self-seeking flatteries with which the French nobles plied him. To them he was not merely a paladin and a protector, but a host. Three times a week he invited a hundred of the émigrés to dinner, — a courtesy particularly welcome to gentlemen whom the lack of money sometimes reduced to a diet of potatoes

and milk. When he walked out, he was met by
women and children who held out their arms, en-
treating him to take them back to their country. His
imagination became overheated. He said proudly
that his *coup d'état* of 1791, in France, would not
succeed less brilliantly than his *coup d'état* in Sweden,
in 1772. He admired in himself the champion of
crowns, the Godfrey de Bouillon of some crusade
on behalf of authority and monarchy, the magnani-
mous sovereign who, having once been protected
by the court of France, was now going to pay his
debt and overpay it. It seemed to him as if he
had already made his entry into Versailles; as if his
valiant troops, with music and waving banners, had
encamped proudly upon that famous Place d'Armes,
so odiously profaned by the lamentable scenes of the
October Days; as if, crowned with laurels, like the
great Condé, he had ascended the marble staircase
amidst acclamations, and that the uniforms of his
Swedish officers, the liberators of the King of France
and Navarre, were repeating themselves in the dazzling Gallery of the Mirrors. In fact, Gustavus was
the almost unique subject of conversation in Germany,
where he figured, not simply as the defender of the
Most Christian King, but as that of all the princes of
the Holy Empire. Open the *Almanach de Gotha* for
1791. The illustrations are devoted almost exclu-
sively to Sweden and its sovereign. He carried things
with a high hand in those petty German courts where
a perfume of feudalism still lingered and the old

régime hedged itself about with all the trappings
of absolutism in miniature. He returned to Stock-
holm at the beginning of August, 1791, and when
holding a grand review there, said he was rehearsing
his future solemn entry into Paris.

Meantime the emigration is redoubling its activity.
It knocks at every door; it turns its steps toward
every capital. A periodical published at Coblentz
under the title, *Journal de la Contre-Révolution*, seriously maintains that two millions of men are advancing to the assistance of the émigrés. If any one
ventures to express a doubt about it, the initiated
whisper in confidence that the troops only march by
night, so as to take the democrats more readily by
surprise. How active these nobles are, so brilliant,
brave, and witty, yet so frivolous and vain, who
turn all things into jest, and who, seeing France
only from a distance, see it badly and make boasts to
which events always give the lie! Let us follow M.
d'Escars in his peregrinations among the petty prince-
doms of Germany, where he finds Versailles and the
Œil-de-Bœuf again, seen through the big end of the
lorgnette. How he enjoyed himself at the court of
the Cardinal Prince-Bishop of Passau! "Come, Monseigneur," he said to him, "the Opera yesterday; to-
day a ball. Who could deny himself such an easy
life? . . . Hardly had the Cardinal and I taken our
places at the end of the hall, when the waltzing began
with a swiftness, the like of which I had never seen
except there and at Vienna. Each lady, after receiv-

ing a favor and a compliment from His Eminence, continued her waltz. It was with a heart penetrated with gratitude and a lively regret that I took leave of such a worthy prelate."

The Prince de Condé, the Comte d'Artois, and the Comte de Provence has each his diplomacy and his court. Negotiations from every quarter weave in and out incessantly. The projected coalition elaborates itself but slowly. The lack of confidence of Louis XVI. in his brothers, the rival influences, mutual jealousies, and conflicting ambitions of the larger courts; the financial embarrassments of the King of Sweden; the difficulty of rousing the great German people to shake off their torpor; the delays and hesitations of England, Catherine II., the Emperor, and the King of Prussia, — all these causes combine to retard the realization of the wishes of the émigrés. But the declaration of Pilnitz comes of a sudden to revive their hopes. After that they think success is certain.

On August 25, 1791, the Emperor Leopold and Frederic William II., King of Prussia, meet at Pilnitz, the summer residence of the court of Saxony. Splendid fêtes are celebrated in their honor. In the midst of a banquet the unexpected arrival of the brilliant Comte d'Artois is announced. Accompanied by Calonne and the Marquis de Bouillé, he comes to plead what he calls the cause of thrones. By force of persistence he attains the famous declaration which, signed on August 27, 1791, was the cause of a war lasting twenty-two years. It is thus expressed: " The Emperor and the King of Prussia, having listened to the desires and representations of Monsieur (the Comte de Provence) and of M. the Comte d'Artois, jointly declare that they consider the present situation of the King of France as a subject of common interest to all European sovereigns. They hope that this interest cannot fail to be acknowledged by all the Powers whose aid is sought for, and that, consequently, they will not refuse to employ, conjointly with the Emperor and the King of Prussia, the most efficacious means, in proportion to their ability, to put the King of France in a condition to consolidate, in perfect freedom, the bases of a monarchical government equally consistent with the rights of sovereigns and the welfare of the French people. Then, and in that case, the aforesaid Majesties have decided to act promptly and in mutual accord to attain the proposed and common end. Meanwhile they will give their troops the necessary orders so that they may be in readiness for action."

The émigrés are beside themselves with joy. They triumph, they proclaim victory. To listen to them, foreign armies are about to invade France immediately. There will be fifty thousand Austrians in Flanders, forty thousand Swiss and as many Piedmontese in Provence and Dauphiny, fifty thousand Prussians on the Rhine; Russia and Sweden will send their fleets under command of M. de Nassau and Gustavus III.; Holland will furnish two millions; Spain and the Two Sicilies will join the coalition. France, add the émigrés, is no longer a military power; its army is without officers, its frontier towns defenceless, its arsenals empty, its magazines unprovisioned.

Near Louis XVI. there is a woman deeply opposed to the Revolution, and sincerely attached to the old régime, but whose sentiments, nevertheless, are far more French than this. It is the pious and courageous Madame Elisabeth. August 5, 1791, she wrote to Madame de Bombelles: "People retail a thousand scraps of news, each of them still more foolish than the others. They say that Russia, Prussia, Sweden, all Germany, Switzerland, and Sardinia are to fall upon us. . . . But rest easy, my Bombe; your country will acquire glory, and that is all. Three hundred thousand National Guards, perfectly organized, and every one a hero by nature, line the frontiers, and will not permit a single Uhlan to come near. The malicious say that near Maubeuge eight Uhlans made five hundred National Guards, with three cannons, beg for mercy. We must let them talk, — it amuses them; our turn will come to mock at them."

As to Marie Antoinette, she said to M. François Hue: "The sudden invasion of foreign troops would cause inevitable disorders. The King's subjects, both good and bad, would infallibly suffer by it. The assistance of foreigners, no matter how friendly they

appear, is one of those measures which a wise king
should not employ save at the last extremity." But,
alas! there were moments when this last extremity
seemed inevitable to her. She spoke of the émigrés with more bitterness than confidence. She
complained of the insubordination of the King's two
brothers. It would have been painful to Louis XVI.
to feel himself indebted to them for the restoration
of his authority. The idea of a regency under the
Comte de Provence seemed to him an attack against
the rights of the crown. He condemned the exag-
gerations of the émigrés, more royalist than the King
himself, and understood better than any one the
futility and frivolity of what went on at Coblentz.
But the situation was becoming so serious, the revolutionary spirit made such progress, and the hapless
sovereign found so much ill-will and ingratitude
among his subjects, that he often cast a glance across
the frontiers. As M. de Lamartine has said, it was
not the King who conspired; it was the man, the husband, and the father, who sought the aid of foreigners
to secure the safety of his wife and children.

It must not be forgotten, moreover, that the
national idea was not so strongly accentuated then
as now. Throughout the entire history of France
we behold sometimes the kings, and sometimes their
subjects, invoking without shame the aid of foreign
armies. The leaguers called in Spanish troops.
Henri IV. conquered his realm by the aid of English troops. Under Louis XIII. the Protestants of

Rochelle were England's allies. At the time of the
Fronde, the great Condé fought against France under
the standards of Spain. After the revocation of the
edict of Nantes the French refugees took service in
the Prussian army. The English in America had
just been asking for French assistance against their
mother country. The monarchical and religious sentiment took precedence of the national sentiment
among the nobility at the end of the eighteenth century. The idea of the throne and the altar out-
weighed that of country. The men at Coblentz did
not consider themselves as compatriots of the Jacobins who were threatening their property, their honor,
and their life. Shall we not see, even in the nine-
teenth century, the heroic soldier of Valmy, the
future Louis-Philippe, asking a commission from the
Spanish Cortes, in the hope of bearing arms against
France?

IV.

ACCEPTANCE OF THE CONSTITUTION.

THE acceptance of the Constitution was like a clear spot in a cloudy sky, though a very brief and not very luminous one. Marie Antoinette pretended to revive to hope. July 30, 1791, she wrote to her brother, the Emperor Leopold, that the influential men of the Assembly had pronounced for the re-establishment of the royal authority, and that everything seemed tending toward the termination of disorder. "It is necessary, therefore," she added, "that nothing shall be done abroad to hinder a salutary tendency. An attempt at armed intervention would be particularly, and from all points of view, to be dreaded." But next day the Queen thus expressed herself in her correspondence with Count Mercy-Argenteau: "I wrote a letter to the Emperor yesterday (the 30th); I should be ashamed of it, if I did not hope that my brother would understand that, in my position, I am obliged to do and to write all that is required of me. It is essential that my brother should send me a circumstantial letter in reply, which might answer as a sort of basis for negotiations here. Send a courier at once to warn him of this." The Abbé Louis (the future Baron Louis, Minister of Finances under the Restoration) went to Brussels with the messages, dictated by Barnave, inviting the émigrés to moderation. The Abbé Louis, who was one of the Constitutional group, was apparently the Queen's envoy. But on August 1, she wrote to Count Mercy-Argenteau: "The Abbé will say that he has been accredited by me to talk with you. It is essential that you shall seem to listen to him and to be prepossessed; but do not allow yourself to be influenced by him. I am obliged to be extremely cautious with him and his friends. They have been useful to me, and at this moment they are so still; but, however good may be the intentions they manifest, their ideas are exaggerated and could never suit us." Even while hoping for something from abroad, Marie Antoinette did not desire an invasion. What she wanted was diplomatic action, an armed Congress. "I always persist," she added, "in wishing that the Powers should treat with an army behind them, but I think it would be extremely dangerous to seem to wish to enter France."

The unhappy Queen, even while simulating confidence, knew very well what to think about the schemes for public regeneration and felicity, from which so much was promised. She had seen the men at work who were going to make France so rich and prosperous. She was edified by what certain people call liberty. She understood the greatness of soul of these philosophers who boasted that they would bring back the age of gold. "These people," said she to Madame Campan, "have no desire for sovereigns. We shall succumb to their perfidious but consistent policy. They are demolishing the monarchy stone by stone."

Meanwhile the rigors of the captivity in the Tuileries were gradually diminishing. Louis XVI., who had been put under arrest like a simple officer, little by little became King again. Certain persons went so far as to claim that he was about to become so altogether. There was talk of creating a guard for him. It was said that he was to be a monarch after the English pattern. The advocates of a parliamentary system were delighted. September 3, 1791, a deputation from the National Assembly came in great pomp to bring to the King, who was still a captive, the Constitutional Act. They set out at seven in the evening, preceded by ushers and torches and marching between a double row of National Guards, and entered the Tuileries by way of the Carrousel. Next day Madame Elisabeth wrote: "The Constitution is finished, and has been in the King's hands since yesterday. To-day the doors were opened. There were many cries of 'Long live the King and the Queen.' At Vespers there was applause when the King entered and went out. He has decided that those who have been guarding him, and also the Queen and his son, shall continue to act as his guard of honor, until the formation of his household.

There are some honest men among them. Nevertheless, the palace is surrounded as usual by four or five
hundred National Guards. Paris is not in commotion. Enormous crowds come to the Tuileries. But
they are all people who make a good enough appearance. Now and then we can see that some of them
are well affected towards us. The others are quiet,
and all seem glad to see their former master, hoping
that he will promptly sign this superb document with
which all their heads are turned, and which they
think was made for their happiness." At the same
time, Marie Antoinette wrote to Count Mercy-Argenteau: " You must surely have received the charter;
it is a tissue of impracticable absurdities. With time
and a little wisdom, I still hope that we may at least
prepare a happier future for our children."

September 13, Louis XVI. addressed to the National Assembly a message, concerted with Barnave,
in which he accepted the new Constitution. "In
order to extinguish animosities," said he in this document, "let us agree to a mutual forgetfulness of the
past. Let the accusations and prosecutions which
have arisen solely from the events of the Revolution
be extinguished by a general reconciliation. I wish
to swear to the Constitution in the very place where
it was made, and I will come to the National Assembly at noon to-morrow." Upon the motion of Lafayette, the Assembly unanimously adopted the general
amnesty asked for by the King, and a numerous
deputation went to carry him this decree, which set

at liberty all who had taken part in the Varennes journey. In the morning of September 14, Madame Elisabeth wrote to Madame de Raigecourt: "I am going to the Assembly at noon, to attend the Queen. If I were the mistress, I certainly would not go. But, I do not know, all this will not cost more to me than to many others, although assuredly I am far from being a Constitutionalist."

The firing of cannon and popular joy announced the arrival of the royal cortège in the Hall of the Manège. Louis XVI. wore no order but the cross of Saint Louis, in deference to a decree of the Assembly which had just abolished all other decorations. It was a curious symptom that the Most Christian King should no longer dare to wear the order of the Holy Spirit. He mounted slowly to the armchair intended for him. At his left, and on the same level, was the seat of the President of the Assembly, de Thouret, who, like the King, was to perish on the scaffold. The Queen, the Dauphin, Madame Royale, and Madame Elisabeth took places in one of the boxes. Hardly had Louis XVI. taken the oath, when the President, in an affected manner, hastily sat down. Louis XVI., who noticed this, also resumed his seat without delay. Subjects sitting down in advance of their sovereign was in the eyes of Louis XVI. and his family the highest pitch of insolence and scandal.

The Assembly reconducted the monarch to his palace. Acclamations resounded on all sides. Salvos of artillery and enthusiastic applause announced the

opening of a new era. But Louis XVI. and his
Queen were sad unto death. On returning from the
Tuileries, the King, looking very pale, entered Marie
Antoinette's apartment. His countenance was extremely altered. Throwing himself into an armchair, he cried, "All is lost!" Then, turning toward
Madame Campan, "Ah! Madame," said he, "you
were a witness of this humiliation. What! you
came to France to see. . . ." And sobs impeded
his utterance. The Queen fell on her knees before
him and clasped him in her arms. "I stayed," adds
Madame Campan, "not through blamable curiosity,
but because I was so stupefied that I could not tell
what I ought to do. The Queen said to me, 'Ah!
go away! go away!' with an accent which meant,
'Do not stay to be a spectator of your sovereign's
prostration and despair.'"

While the republicans and Orleanists were celebrating the new Constitution, the royalists who were
faithful to Louis XVI. amused themselves by snatch-
ing some ephemeral triumphs in the theatres. At
the Nation Theatre they got *Gaston et Bayard* and
La Partie de chasse de Henri IV. produced on September 16. After having frantically applauded the
passages which make allusion to the ancient love of
the French people for their king, they went everywhere repeating, "Public opinion is changed; the
Constitution will not last." They paid men and
women of the people to cry "Long live the King!"
"Long live the Queen!" beneath the windows of the

Tuileries. And they assured Louis XVI. that, the Assembly once dissolved, the monarchical sentiment would at once resume its vigor.

The Constitution was solemnly proclaimed on September 18, in the midst of a magnificent fête in the Champ-de-Mars. The citizens embraced each other like brethren. The new Constitution was read from the summit of the Altar of the Country. Balloons displaying patriotic inscriptions were sent up in the Champs-Élysées. The aëronauts threw down pamphlets of the Constitution on the heads of the crowd. In the evening the illuminations were superb. Garlands of fire, reaching from tree to tree, outlined a sparkling avenue from the Barrière de l'Étoile to the Tuileries, in which numerous bands played joyous music. At eleven o'clock, Louis XVI. and his family drove in a carriage through this radiant avenue. The acclamations were enthusiastic. The ungrateful nation could not get over its habit of crying, "Long live the King!" For one moment the bitterest revolutionists, the most enthusiastic republicans, became royalists in spite of themselves. The same Champs-Élysées which three months before had been a road of humiliation and of anguish was transformed into a triumphal way. It was like a magic souvenir — an evocation of the happy days. The lamp-posts were alight, and this time no victims were hanging from them. Marie Antoinette could not believe that they were the same people. What! they had still homage and benedictions for her? What! cries of "Long live

the Queen!" resounded once more? But, like the
slave in ancient triumphs, there was a man of the people who disturbed the joy of this ovation. Every time
that the acclamations ceased, this man, who never
quitted the door of the royal carriage for an instant,
cried out alone, and with the voice of a stentor: "Do
not believe them. Long live the Nation!" And
this sinister personage froze Marie Antoinette with
terror.

However, there was a few days' lull in the storm.
The royal family reappeared in the theatres and were
applauded as of old. "We have been at the Opéra,"
wrote Madame Elisabeth, September 25. " To-morrow we are going to the Comédie. I am enchanted
about it; and to-day we had a *Te Deum* during the
Mass. There was one also at Notre Dame. Monseigneur the intruder (Gobel, the Constitutional
Bishop of Paris) was very anxious that we should go
there. But when one is sung at home, one is dis-
pensed from going to find another elsewhere. We
kept quiet, therefore. This evening we are to have
another illumination. The garden will be superb,
all hung with lamps and those little glass things
which for two years no one has been able to name
without horror."

September 30, Louis XVI. went to the Hall of
the Manège, to be present at the closing session of
the Constituent Assembly. Bailly, in the name
of the municipality, and M. de Pastoret, in the name
of the departments, congratulated it on the achieve-

ment of its task. "Legislators," said Bailly, "you have been armed with the greatest power with which men can be invested. To-morrow you will again be nothing. It is neither interest nor flattery, then, which praises you. It is your works. We announce to you the benedictions of posterity, which for you begin to-day." "Liberty," said M. de Pastoret afterwards, "had fled over seas, or taken refuge in the mountains. You have raised up again its shattered throne. Despotism had effaced all the pages of the book of Nature. You have established anew the Decalogue of free men." The King left the hall amid the huzzas and acclamations of the Assembly and the galleries. The President then said, "The National Constituent Assembly declares that it has fulfilled its mission, and that all its sessions are over." It was four o'clock in the afternoon.

When Robespierre and Pétion went out, the crowd crowned them with oak leaves and took the horses out of their carriage to drag them in triumph. They called one of them the Incorruptible, and the other the Virtuous. This ovation to the two tribunes presaged the future, and through '91 pierced already '93.

In reality, nobody laid down his arms. All Paris was joyful. The bells rang. Fêtes were given. They sang. They illuminated. But none of these demonstrations of gaiety deceived the sagacious observer. As a matter of fact, the acceptance of the

Constitution, far from reuniting minds, divided them
more than ever. The journals redoubled their violence. The cafés were like fields of battle. The
reactionists who said, "Out of the old régime there
is no salvation," considered the new Constitution a
miserable scrap of paper, a tissue of criminal absurdities. Those who thought that Louis XVI. might
have accepted it in good faith, regarded him as a
ridiculous sovereign, the phantom of a king, pro-
nouncing his own deposition. An officer of dragoons
at a table d'hôte cried, as he shivered his glass, "I
am a royalist, but I am not a *Louis seiziste*."

But, to the majority of the King's partisans, his acceptance was merely a feint, a means of gaining time.
"It is necessary," said they, "that Louis XVI. should
pretend to be pleased with everything, that he should
sign whatever is presented to him, that he should aston-
ish the Constitutionals by his submission and docil-
ity."

They added that if Monsieur were declared regent
and the Count d'Artois lieutenant-general of the
realm, the King ought to be, as in effect he was, absolutely null, eclipsed, annihilated, for the time
being. Otherwise, the attitude of the Princes could
not be justified. And again they said: "Things will
right themselves. The parliamentary phantasma-
goria will disappear in an instant. It is a soap
bubble which will vanish into air."

"Distrust! Distrust!" shrieked the Jacobins.
They were more suspicious, more atrabilious than

ever. Louis XVI. is going to essay in good faith
his rôle as a constitutional sovereign. But the contract is synallagmatic, two-sided. That the King
may be loyal to the Constitution, it is necessary that
his subjects shall be loyal to him; the royal prerogatives, and notably the right of *veto*, must be respected; the Constitution must be something different
from an instrument of anarchy and disorder. The
Constitutional party, honorable men in spite of their
illusions, would like a fair and honest trial. But the
Constitutionals are already out of the running. Barnave, who was in advance of Mirabeau, is now dis-
tanced by a swarm of democrats, who see in him
nothing but a belated conservative. It is all over
with moderation. There is no place for anything
but violence. The drama which was supposed to be
finished, has just begun. The Constitution is not
the epilogue; it is the prologue; and Louis XVI. and
Marie Antoinette are covered with flowers only to
make them resemble the victims of antiquity before
leading them to the sacrifice.

V.

MARIE ANTOINETTE'S LAST EVENINGS AT THE THEATRE.

WHEN I was at the Odéon, watching a play in which Marie Antoinette comes on the scene, I looked at the place where the Sovereign often made her appearance in this hall where the Théâtre Français was installed at the end of the old régime, and where the first representation of the *Mariage de Figaro* was given. I saw again the splendid toilets, the high coiffures, and precious stones; I breathed that perfume of elegance which is found no more. It seemed to me that I saw the Queen, not on the stage where they were trying to represent her, but in her box, surrounded by her maids of honor and her chamberlains, saluted on coming in and going out by acclamations from the whole theatre, and giving with her own royal hand throughout the play the signals for applause.

In 1791 the appearance of the Queen still produced a great effect upon the public. But there was no longer the same unanimity of enthusiasm. The Revolution had insinuated itself everywhere, in salons and theatres as well as in the streets and

264

public places. The Jacobins sent emissaries to the pit as well as to the galleries of the National Assembly. Dramatic representations gave perpetual opportunities for insults and contests between parties. Marie Antoinette, who had great courage, was not afraid to brave the popular tiger. In appearing before the crowd, where she found so many enemies, she accustomed herself to face her persecutors, soon to be her tormentors. She tried to avail herself once more of that prestige which not long ago had procured her so much reverence. She wanted to see whether the power of her beauty, joined to the new majesty of her sorrow, would not still affect an ungrateful people. Every evening spent at the theatre was like a battle given courageously to calumny and insult. When she set her foot in one, she did not know whether she should leave it without hearing criticisms or curses levelled at her; and when her coming was again greeted with applause, when she beheld traces of emotion and respect on different faces, she returned to the Tuileries with a smile on her lips and gratitude in the depths of her heart.

She had not been to the theatre in a long time, but in September, 1791, she decided to go as a sort of proof of her confidence in the Parisians. At this time, Louis XVI. and Marie Antoinette gained a renewal of popularity. The National Assembly in its session chamber might fail in respect toward the Sovereign; but the people followed him with huzzas in the streets. " With the disposition of the French

people to idolatry," said Prudhomme at this time, in
his *Journal des Révolutions de Paris*, "such a king
would soon be only the father of the subjects of the
State, and from such paternity to despotism is only
a step. Let us avoid enthusiasm." At the fête
given on September 18, 1791, the affection of the
people for Louis XVI. approached delirium, and at
the one given in the garden of the Tuileries on the
25th of the same month it rose to ecstasy. "It was
useless for the orchestra to play the favorite air *Ça
ira*," said Prudhomme again; "it would not do; they
had to repeat royalist ditties."

Madame Elisabeth wrote to Madame de Raigecourt, September 25: "We have been to the Opéra,
and to-morrow we are going to the Comédie. What
pleasures! I am perfectly enchanted with them."
Madame Campan has said of these two representations: "Their Majesties were at the Opéra. The
assembly was composed of all those who adhered
to the King's party, and on that day one could
enjoy the happiness of seeing him surrounded by
faithful subjects: the plaudits were sincere. At
the Français the play chosen was the *Coquette cor-
rigée*, simply because Mademoiselle Contat made
her greatest success in it. Nevertheless, as the title
of the piece continually suggested to my mind the
opinion which the Queen's enemies had spread concerning her, I found the selection injudicious without
knowing how to say so to Her Majesty. But sincere
attachment gives courage; I explained myself; she

took it kindly, and requested a different play: they gave *La Gouvernante.* The Queen, Madame the King's daughter, and Madame Elisabeth were all very well received. It is true that the opinions and sentiments of the spectators could not but be favorable; care had been taken, before each of these representations, to fill the pit properly."

On October 8 the royal family went to the Théâtre Italien. This theatre was on the boulevard which has borrowed its name, just opposite the rue de Richelieu. It was built in 1783, on the site of the Hôtel Choiseul, for the so-called actors of the Comédie Italienne, who had been united, since 1762, with those of the Opéra Comique. They were to represent there "French comedies, comic operas, and musical performances, whether vaudevilles, ariettas, or burlesques." The evening of October 8, 1791, was particularly touching. The theatre resounded more than once with acclamations, blended sometimes with sobs; tenderness united with respect. Nor was the enthusiasm less in the approaches to the theatre than within the walls. The populace became itself again; that is to say, gentle, compassionate, full of veneration for the King and his family. Louis XVI. and Marie Antoinette were happy to be able to show the Dauphin and his sister this crowd whom the two children had seen so hostile through the dust of the tumultuous return from Varennes. Madame Elisabeth wrote Madame de Raigecourt, October 12: "All is tranquil here; but who knows how long it will

last? I think it will be long, because, as the people
do not meet with any resistance, they have no reason
to become exasperated. At this moment the King is
the object of public adoration. You can form no
idea of the uproar at the Comédie Italienne last
Saturday; but it remains to be seen how long this
enthusiasm will last!"

At this time, Marie Antoinette, usually so calumniated, herself regained popularity. The *Correspon-
dance secrète sur la cour et la ville*, from 1777 to 1791,
published by M. de Lescure from manuscripts in the
imperial library of Saint Petersburg, contains a very
curious passage on this change of opinion:—

"*December* 30, 1791.—The King makes every
effort to recover his popularity. He often walks in
the city, and especially in the suburbs, but it is sufficiently remarkable that he has never received as
much applause as was given to the Queen yesterday
at the Opéra.[1] The people shouted a thousand times,
the women above all, 'Long live the Queen!' afterwards, 'Long live the Nation!' and very seldom,
'Long live the King!' It begins to dawn on the
public that this Princess, whose will and whose reso-
lutions are firm and decided, has resolved in good
faith to adhere to the Constitution, which assures us
of the neutrality of the Emperor, while Louis XVI.
regrets the old régime."

But the good dispositions of the multitude toward

---

[1] The Opéra was at this time installed in the boulevard, in the
hall which was afterward the theatre of the Porte Saint Martin.

the Queen were not to be very lasting. The Jacobins especially feared public sympathy. They were not slow in organizing counter-demonstrations. Yet Marie Antoinette was once more applauded at the theatre: it was at the Italiens, on February 20, 1792. But on that evening the ovations were contested. There was a struggle, and, in order to triumph, the partisans of the royal family were obliged to display all their zeal and devotion.

The play was one which lent itself to allusions to monarchical faith and fidelity: Grétry's comic opera, *Les Événements imprévus*, in which the charming cantatrice, Madame Dugazon, was then performing wonders. She was royalist at heart. She wished to try the public that evening. According to Madame Campan's account, she was seen to bow towards the Queen when singing these words in a duet: "Ah, how I love my mistress!" At once, more than a score of voices shouted from the pit: "No mistress! no master! Liberty!" A number of men in the boxes and balconies responded: "Long live the Queen! Long live the King! May the King and Queen live forever!" The pit answered: "No master! no Queen!" The quarrel grew hotter, the pit divided into two parties which fought together, and the Jacobins got the worst of it. Tufts of their black hair were flying all over the theatre. (They alone, at this epoch, had abandoned the custom of powdering their hair.)

A large number of the guards arrived. The Faubourg Saint-Antoine, apprised of what was going on at the Italiens, had assembled and were already talking of marching toward the theatre. The Queen preserved the noblest and most calm demeanor; the officers of the guard surrounded and reassured her. Their behavior was active and prudent, and no bad result followed. On going out, the Queen was greatly applauded. It was the last time that she entered a theatre. During the whole evening her attitude had been profoundly touching. With the exception of the Jacobins, all the spectators sympathized with her. More than once she dried her eyes. Even the applause saddened her. The Dauphin, who sat on her lap, seemed to be asking why she wept. And she seemed to be answering and seeking to tranquillize him.

This evening of February 20, 1792, was to be the Queen's last ovation. Madame Elisabeth wrote to Madame de Raigecourt on February 22: "The Queen and her children were at the Comédie yesterday. There was an infernal racket of applause. Jacobins wanted to make an uproar, but they were beaten. The duet in the *Événements imprévus* between the valet and the chambermaid, concerning their love for their master and mistress, was encored four times; and when it came to the words, 'We must make them happy,' nearly the whole theatre cried, 'Yes! yes!' Can you understand our nation? It must be owned, it has charming moments. Whereupon I wish you good night, and beg you to pray God well during this Lent that He may look mercifully

on us. But, my heart, take care to think only of
His glory, and put aside all which relates to the
world. I embrace you."

Madame Elisabeth spoke of the same evening in
a letter which she wrote on February 23, to her
brother, the Count d'Artois : " Paris is almost tranquil. The other day at the Comédie, when the
Queen was there with her children, there was an
infernal racket which ended in an astonishing scene
by which a great many persons were affected. The
majority of those present shouted, 'Long live the
King! Long live the Queen!' enough to bring the
roof down. Those who were of a different mind were
beaten, and a duet which suggested a reconciliation
was repeated four times. But it was only a moment,
one of those gleams which the nation has sometimes,
and God knows whether it will continue."

No ; it will not continue. On the next day after
that evening of February 20, the *Orateur du peuple*
newspaper wrote: " The Queen shall be flogged in
her box at the theatre. The Queen is playing the
harlot." What follows is not fit to be quoted. The
Queen was never to appear in a theatre again. Her
brother's death was near, and the mourning she was
about to wear was not the mourning of the Emperor
Leopold alone, but that of the French monarchy and
its ancient and venerable glories.

VI.

AT the close of 1791, Louis XVI. and the Duke of Orleans were very near a reconciliation. The Duke remembered now and then that he was a Bourbon and a Prince of the blood. At such times he repented of his errors; he had an intuition of his duties; he thought seriously of behaving like a good kinsman toward the King; but a sort of fatality flung him back into his usual faults, and the first Prince of the blood again became seditious. This happened once again after the acceptance of the Constitution. Thinking of conciliation and clemency, Louis XVI. appointed his cousin admiral, on September 16, 1791, and the Duke went to thank the Minister of Marine, M. Bertrand de Molleville, who has recounted in his Memoirs the details of his interview with the Prince.

The Duke of Orleans assured the Minister, in a tone of perfect frankness and loyalty, that he valued extremely the favor the King had granted him, because it would enable him to show His Majesty how greatly he had been calumniated. "I am very unfortunate," said he, "without deserving to be so. They have laid a thousand atrocities at my door, of which I am absolutely innocent. I have been supposed guilty, solely because I have disdained to clear myself of crimes which I hold in the profoundest horror. You are the first minister to whom I have said as much, because you are the first whose character has always inspired me with confidence. You will presently have a favorable opportunity to judge whether my conduct gives the lie to my words." M. Bertrand de Molleville replied: "Monseigneur, I so greatly fear to weaken the force of your remarks in reporting them to the King, as you desire, that I beg you to express your sentiments to His Majesty yourself." "That is precisely what I desire," returned the Duke; "and if I could flatter myself that the King would receive me, I would go to him to-morrow."

That very evening, at the council, the Minister gave the King an account of the visit of the Duke of Orleans. Louis XVI. concluded to receive his cousin; and on the following day had a conversation with him for more than half an hour, with which he appeared satisfied. He said afterwards to M. Bertrand de Molleville: "I agree with you; he comes back to us sincerely, and will do all in his power to repair the evils done in his name, and in which it is possible that he has had less share than we have supposed."

The reconciliation had seemed to be complete.

But what occurred on the following Sunday destroyed all its effects, and the abyss, instead of being covered up, yawned again as wide as ever. On that day the Duke came to the Tuileries to be present at the King's levee. The interview between Louis XVI. and his cousin had not been made known, and hence the appearance of the Prince caused general surprise. The courtiers saw in it not an evidence of submission, but an act of mere bravado. In their eyes, the Duke of Orleans was the most dangerous and guiltiest of revolutionists. They attributed all catastrophes and all crimes to him. His presence made them cry out with horror; and they pressed around him, affecting to tread on his toes, and pushed him toward the door. Not being able to reach the King's chamber, he went to the apartment of the Queen. The table was already laid. Some one cried out, "Let nobody go near the dishes!" as if to insinuate that the Prince might poison them. Ironical whispers and murmurs of indignation forced him to retire without having seen a single member of the royal family. He regained the stairway, intending to go out. As he was descending the steps, somebody spat, over the banisters, on his clothes and his head. An eye-witness of this scene, Bertrand de Molleville, adds, in his Memoirs: "The Duke of Orleans hastened out of the palace, with rage and indignation in his heart, and convinced that he owed these outrages to the King and Queen, who were not only ignorant of them, but were extremely angry when they were told. From that moment he abandoned himself entirely to an implacable hatred, and swore to revenge himself. Frightful oath, to which he has been only too faithful."

Yesterday a royalist, and a republican to-day, discontented with others and with himself, drawn by the fascination of the abyss, and sinking gradually into the gulf of false situations, a nobleman astray, a Jacobin prince, the tormentors will turn him to account before making him their victim. Sad fatality of circumstances! At another epoch the Duke, who is amiable and witty, would be loved and honored. Why was he born in this confused and troubled period which destroys the very notion of right and duty? One might say he had a presentiment of his faults and their expiation. Sometimes he tries to leave the scorching arena which will be so fatal to him, and again he comes back to it, pushed as it were by an irresistible force. He takes the first step toward a reconciliation with his King, and he is discouraged and prevented from making the second. Then, in vexation, he goes back into extremes. He will seek the elements of his vengeance in the lower depths of society. He will pick up his weapons out of the mud. He will subsidize men who to-day will demand his gold and to-morrow his head. Because he cannot be the familiar of the Tuileries, he becomes the courtier of the Jacobin club.

This used-up man, weary of enjoyment, satiated with luxury, gold, and pleasure, finds perhaps a cer-

tain amusement in the unhealthy but violent emotions
of the revolutionary crisis. In London, with his enormous fortune, he could live quietly, without danger
and without responsibility, out of the reach of tempests. But though he may assure his friend, Mrs.
Elliot, that he has always envied the position of an
English country gentleman, and instead of wishing
to make himself king, as his enemies declare, he
would willingly exchange his position and his fortune
for a small estate in England and the privileges of
that agreeable country, yet he prefers, in spite of
everything, to remain on the battle-field of insurrection, in the furnace, in the crater of this volcanic
Paris, where his palace is the rendezvous of all the
revolutionary bands, and the focus of all conspiracies.
There kennels of debauchery swarm close beside the
splendors of elegance and riches. He lives there,
surrounded by the strangest of courts. Noblemen
who have come down in the world elbow, in his
salons, revolutionists starving when they ask for
money, insolent when they have received it. When
one accosts the Duke, one is tempted to say to him,
" Is it to the Prince of the blood that I address myself, or to the Jacobin? "

This personage of many faces has something in
him which troubles and disquiets. His destiny is an
enigma of which one cannot find the word. Is he a
republican or a royalist, a traitor or a patriot? Does
he act deliberately, or does he let himself drift at the
mercy of the stream? Are his morning thoughts

what his evening thoughts were? Is he not change
itself, in politics as in love? Has he not lost free
will? Is he not all the more a slave, that his mistress
calls herself Liberty?

Each day the spectacles presented by events are so
singular, so unforeseen; things march so fast; the
excitement is so terrible; that it is much if the Duke
of Orleans recognizes himself, if he keeps the consciousness of his identity. His new rôle resembles
the old one so little, that there is in his very person
something like a metamorphosis, an avatar. The
time is approaching when people will ask themselves
whether citizen Philippe-Égalité is really the same
person as Louis Joseph, Duke of Orleans, head of the
younger branch of the Bourbons, first Prince of the
blood, descendant in the direct line of Saint Louis
and Henri IV. Yes, the time is coming when Ser-
gent, member of the Council General, will write:
"I saw the Duke of Orleans shrug his shoulders on
receiving the name of Égalité, which was given him
by Manuel, procureur of the Commune of Paris. He
spoke to me about it with an ironical pity when, on
coming out of the Hôtel-de-Ville together, where I
happened to be at the moment, I said to him, laugh-
ing: 'How well that suits you! The name of a
nymph for you, a colonel of hussars with black mous-
taches!' He replied: 'You will do me the justice
to believe that I did not come to the Commune to
change my names, and that this one was imposed on
me. You heard the galleries applauding that stupid

Manuel. What could I do or say? I came to petition
for my daughter, who was about to be declared an
émigrée, and I had to sacrifice to that important
affair my repugnance to this name, a burlesque for
me.'"

The destiny of the Duke of Orleans is a lesson
which cannot be too deeply pondered. No person in
history shows in a more striking manner what the
revolutionary gearing really is. Camille Desmoulins,
in his *Fragments de l'histoire secrète de la Révolution*,
has written: "It would be very singular if Philippe
d'Orléans did not belong to the Orleans faction; but
the thing is not impossible." That is not a paradox.
The Prince was not the chief of his partisans; he was
their plaything and their victim. "The Duke of
Orleans," says Mrs. Elliot in her Memoirs, "was a
very amiable man, of great distinction in manners,
and of a pliant character, but the least suitable man
that ever lived for the position of chief of a great
faction. Neither his mind, his talents, nor even his
education, rendered him fit to play such a part.
Laclos was the cause of all the crimes attributed to
the Orleans faction, and I am very sure that the
Duke knew very little about what was done in his
name."

Mrs. Elliot describes this Prince as loving pleasure
above all things; unable to endure work or business
of any sort; never reading, nor doing anything but
amuse himself; madly in love with Madame de
Buffon, whom he drove about all day in an open

carriage, and took to all the sights in the evenings.
"The misfortune of the Duke," adds the beautiful
Englishwoman, "was to be surrounded by ambitious
persons, who led him by degrees to their own ends,
pushing him on until he found himself too much
in their power to draw back. His partisans were
enchanted when a new insult had been offered him
at the court, for they saw very well that they had
nothing more to fear from that quarter." Before
that his faction was always afraid lest he might be
treated better at the Tuileries, and so might slip
through their fingers.

The Orleanist conspiracies were not the work of
the Duke of Orleans. He had only the shame and
grief of submitting to them. At the time of the
flight to Varennes, nothing would have been easier for
him than to intrigue for the crown. Instead of doing
so, he said, "So long as the King is in the country,
he alone is king." June 26, 1791, he renounced the
right to the regency given him by the Constitution.
"It is no longer permissible for me," he wrote at that
time, "to leave the simple citizen class, which I did
not enter without the firm determination to remain
in it forever; and in me ambition would be an inex-
cusable inconsequence."

Was that the language of a hypocrite? We do
not think so. Whoever, at this epoch, should have
predicted to the Duke that he would soon be a regicide, would have made him shrug his shoulders.

Unhappily, evil influences were multiplying daily

around the ill-fated Prince; and his wife, the virtuous
daughter of the venerable Duke de Penthièvre, was
no longer at his side to counterbalance them. This
exemplary Princess, who had married for love, and
given her husband five children, thought herself
unable to palliate by her presence infidelities which
were becoming too public and too scandalous. Quitting the Palais Royal in 1784, she took refuge with
her father; and from that time the Duke gave himself over, body and soul, to those degraded women
who are as fond of disorder in politics as in the
family, and who imagined that the Revolution would
avenge them for the contempt they inspired in society.
The Dantons, the Héberts, the Marats, would never
have gained a hold on a prince who had remained
faithful to such a woman as the Duchess of Orleans.

Involved, almost in spite of himself, in the demagogic vortex, the Duke will sometimes wish to extri-
cate himself. A secret voice will cry to him, Go on!
He will try in vain to take precautions against his
natural impulses. Fatality will everywhere pursue
him. At the commencement of 1792 he would be
glad to take refuge, like his sons, the Dukes of Chartres and Montpensier, in that asylum of patriotism
and honor, the army. But hardly has he done so
when he is refused permission to remain. Then he
will ask for a naval command. The ship he wants
to embark on will not return to France until the
close of 1793. Had the request of the Prince been
acceded to, he would have been neither a member of

the Convention nor a regicide.   But his evil star
keeps him in this fatal Paris, where the King's scaffold and his own are going to be erected.   One
might say that some mysterious force is pushing him
toward the abyss.   It is only by a sort of chance that
he will be elected to the Convention, in which he
is to play such a melancholy rôle.   The twenty-three
first deputies of Paris were chosen on September 18,
1792.   There was but one more to be elected.   The
twenty-fourth will be the Duke of Orleans.   He will
have only the strictly necessary majority.   One vote
less, and he would not have been elected, and his
memory would not have borne an ineffaceable stain.

It is at this time that he will ask Mrs. Elliot if she
thinks him vile enough to be able to pass through
the streets of Paris without unhappiness.   Then she
will implore him " to get out of the hands of all
these vile beings who surround him, and not allow
the wretches to use his name as a screen for such horrible deeds."   The Prince will answer: " That seems
a very easy thing to do in your salon; I would be
very glad if it were as easy in reality.   But I am in
the stream, and find myself obliged to follow it.   I
am no longer master of myself or of my name."

VII.

THE RETURN OF THE PRINCESS DE LAMBALLE TO
THE TUILERIES.

IT was not alone the middle classes and the people
who afflicted Louis XVI. and Marie Antoinette.
The nobility also chagrined them deeply. The very
men who had carried liberalism to all lengths, who
had been Voltairians and revolutionists of the worst
sort, who had wilfully cast off their titles and privileges as out of date and worthless, bitterly reproached
the King with the destruction of the old régime.
This great lady, a fanatical admirer of Rousseau's
Contrat Social, could not be reconciled to the slightest
changes in point of etiquette. That great lord, a
disciple of Helvétius and Baron d'Holbach, bore
malice against Louis XVI. on account of the attacks
made on the Catholic religion. The nobles who had
done most to bring about the triumph of the new
ideas, emigrated, and left the unfortunate monarch
to bear the consequences of their own conduct.
Others remained in France only to pay court to the
Jacobins. As M. Granier de Cassagnac has said in
his *Histoire des Causes de la Révolution française* :
"One of the most ignoble spectacles which it has

fallen to history to chronicle was witnessed at this
time. Families that for a thousand years had lived
by feudal privileges, and men who for two years had
rejected with unsupportable arrogance the liberal
reforms of Louis XVI. and the equalizing of public
burdens, outdid the Jacobins, whose approbation they
coveted, by demanding that coats-of-arms and liveries
should be abolished. They had used and abused the
institutions of the old France, so long as they provided them with wealth and honors; but now, when
these institutions merely brought them into increasing disfavor with the populace, they rejected them in
cowardly fashion, and replaced the ducal mantle by
the revolutionary jacket, because they could make it
pay them better! Why, then, had they not laid aside
their titles, destroyed their liveries, and effaced their
escutcheons two years sooner? It was because, two
years before, their titles, their liveries, and their
escutcheons had given them precedence, honors,
and salaries at court; but now that the court was
poor and the monarchy disarmed, these beggarly
nobles decorated their ingratitude with the name of
philosophy, and made themselves courtiers of the
people, since they could no longer be profitably the
courtiers of the King." The aristocracy bewailed
the destruction which was their own work. In
spite of all the measures in which they had taken
the initiative, they were surprised that the new
Constitution suppressed what was called rank at
court, and the prerogatives belonging to it. The

Duchess de Duras sent in her resignation as lady of the palace, because she would not yield her right to sit down in the presence of her sovereign. Several more great ladies deserted the Tuileries on the same account. This conduct saddened Marie Antoinette, who saw herself abandoned for the sake of petty privileges at a time when the rights of the crown were so gravely compromised and so violently attacked. She said: "Perhaps I might have found some excuse for the nobility, if at any time I had had the courage to displease them; but I have not. When we are forced to take a step which wounds them, I am sulked at; no one will come to my card-party; the King's evening reception is deserted. They are not willing to consider political necessities; they punish us for our misfortunes."

When the ill-fated Sovereign found so much in-gratitude, inconsistency, levity, and selfishness among the nobility; when she was blamed, accused, and abandoned by the very persons who should have pitied and assisted her the most, it was a great con-solation to meet a soul so pure, disinterested, devoted, and courageous as that of the Princess de Lamballe.

The Princess had been apprised beforehand of the journey to Varennes. It was agreed that in order to avert suspicion, she should go to Aumale, where her father-in-law, the venerable Duke de Penthièvre, had been staying for some time on account of his health. At six in the evening of June 21, 1791, a post-chaise driven at full speed drew up before the house of the

bailiff of Aumale, where M. de Penthièvre was lodg-
ing. The Princess de Lamballe, in great emotion,
hastily alighted from the carriage and was at once
met by her father-in-law and her sister-in-law, the
Duchess of Orleans, who were surprised by this unforeseen arrival. The Princess laid her fingers on
her lips, but as soon as they were alone she acquainted
them with the flight of the royal family, which had
necessitated her own. After a few minutes she
started on again, with fresh horses, to embark for
England at Boulogne. The ship she sailed in had
barely reached the open sea, when a discharge of
cannon from the city announced the King's flight.
A little later, and she would have been detained a
prisoner.

The Princess de Lamballe was entrusted with an
important and difficult mission in England. She
was to attempt to lessen the hostility which the
government displayed toward Louis XVI., and the
secret encouragement given by Pitt to the French
revolutionists. Madame Campan relates that Marie
Antoinette said to her: " I never pronounce the
name of Pitt without a shiver running down my
back. That man is the mortal enemy of France. He
is taking a cruel revenge for the impolitic assistance
given to the American insurgents by the cabinet of
Versailles. He wishes, by our destruction, to guar-
antee forever the maritime power of his own country
from the efforts the King has made to build up his
navy. Pitt has aided the French Revolution from

the very beginning. He will probably continue to
do so until we are completely destroyed."

With all her zeal, the Princess de Lamballe could
obtain nothing from Pitt but a vague promise not
to let the French monarchy perish, because, according
to his own admission, "it would be a great fault
against the tranquillity of all Europe to permit the
revolutionary spirit to bring about a republic in
France." Concerning this remark, Marie Antoinette
said: "Every time that Pitt has declared himself on
the necessity of maintaining a monarchy in France,
he has kept the most absolute silence on what con-
cerns the monarch. These conversations can have
no good result."

Her mission once concluded, the Princess de Lamballe had no thought except that of returning to the
Queen. As she had a presentiment of the dangers
she was about to incur, she made her will. It is
dated October 15, 1791, and breathes the tenderness
of a last adieu as well as the sublime resignation of
a soul awaiting martyrdom. "I entreat the Queen,"
is said in it, "to receive a mark of gratitude from
her to whom she has given the title of her friend, —
a precious title which has formed the happiness of my
life, and which I have never abused except to give
her testimonies of attachment and proofs of my sentiments toward her person, which I have always loved
and cherished till my latest breath. I ask her as a
last favor to accept my alarum watch, to remind her
of the hours we have passed together."

Marie Antoinette was profoundly touched by Madame de Lamballe's devotion. Instead of seeking a tranquil asylum in England or Germany, she was bent on returning to France, and throwing herself into the furnace. But the unhappy Queen repelled this heroic sacrifice, and begged Madame de Lamballe not to make it. In September, 1791, she wrote to her: "Do not return; there would be too much to grieve you in the present state of our affairs. I know well that you are good, and a true friend, and from the depths of my own affection I forbid you to return hither. Wait for the results of the Constitution. Adieu, my dear Lamballe, and believe that my tender friendship for you will end only with my life." But Madame de Lamballe hastened none the less to the post of danger. At the very moment when she entered France, the Queen wrote to her: "No, I repeat it, my dear Lamballe, do not return to us at present; my friendship for you is too greatly alarmed; affairs do not seem to be taking a better turn notwithstanding the acceptance of the Constitution, on which I counted. Stay with good M. de Penthièvre, who has such need of your attention. . . . God grant that time may bring about a change for the better; but the wicked have spread about so many atrocious calumnies that I rely more on my courage than on events. Adieu, then, my dear Lamballe. Be sure that whether you are here or far away, I love you and am sure of your affection." But it was in vain that Marie Antoinette implored

the Princess not to throw herself into the tiger's
jaws. The greater the peril was, the more enthusiastic was her haste to brave it. Madame de Lamballe reached her father-in-law, at Anet, November
14, 1791, and, departing on the 18th, went straight to
Paris. The Duke de Penthièvre said at the time:
" I praise greatly the attachment of my daughter-in-
law for the Queen. She has made a very great sacrifice in order to return to her. I tremble lest she fall
a victim to it."

The merit of the Princess de Lamballe was all the
greater, since it was not honors, but danger, she was
seeking. It was only out of kindness that she performed her functions as superintendent. The offices
of the court were suppressed, and the King was putting off indefinitely the formation of his new civil
household. He was reluctant to choose among those
proposed to him, and to surround himself with persons
devoted to the Revolution. " I know very well," he
said to M. Bertrand de Molleville, " that the Queen
cannot advantageously retain the wives of émigrés near her person, and I have already spoken
to her about it; but on the other hand, it cannot be
expected that she should associate with Mesdames
Pétion, Condorcet, and others of that sort. As for
me, the majority of those whose attendance was formerly most agreeable, have abandoned me, and among
those who remain, there are some who are the torment
of my life." The King and Queen did not desire a
civil household, lest the new names given to the

offices should make evident the abolition of the old
ones; they disliked, moreover, to admit to the most
distinguished employments people who were not
capable of fulfilling them. " If this Constitutional
establishment were formed," said Marie Antoinette,
" there would not be a single noble left near us; and
if things should change, it would be necessary to dis-
miss the people whom we had admitted in their
places."

The court was no longer more than the shadow of
itself. The abode of pleasure was transformed into
a place of anxiety, deception, and grief. It was
feared that the King and Queen might be poisoned,
and a multitude of precautions had to be taken at
each of their meals. Madame Elisabeth wrote to
Madame de Raigecourt, November 16, 1791: "A
droll thing happened during the last few days. A
corporal invented an order to confine the King and
Queen in their apartments from nine o'clock at night
until nine in the morning. This confinement had
lasted for two days before any one heard of it; finally,
on the third day, a grenadier told his captain. The
entire guard was furious; there was going to be a
council of war. According to rule, the corporal ought
to be hanged; but I do not think he will be, and I
should be very sorry if he were. The King was to go
out riding the other day; it was villainous weather,
and he stayed at home; hence, a rumor throughout
Paris that he is again under arrest." This is what
the heir of Louis XIV. had come to. Was it not very

praiseworthy, then, in the Princess de Lamballe to come and shut herself up in this Palace of the Tuileries, where the year 1791 was ending so dismally? She occupied the ground-floor of the Pavilion of Flora, below the apartment of Madame Elisabeth. To the Queen these two admirable women were friends who pushed sacrifice to heroism. Nothing is more affecting than such courage united to such sweetness. Amid the victims of the Revolution, Madame Elisabeth and Madame de Lamballe are lambs without spot. Their ideal suavity brings them into strong contrast with the sanguinary hordes who transform Paris into a pandemonium. They are two angels of consolation in a hell.

INDEX.

FAMOUS WOMEN OF THE
FRENCH COURT.

WITHIN the past few years M. Imbert de Saint-Amand
has written a series of volumes which have made
him one of the most popular authors of France. Each has
for its nucleus some portion of the life of one of the eminent
women who have presided over or figured at the French
court, either at Versailles or the Tuileries. But though thus
largely biographical and possessing the interest inseparable
from personality, the volumes are equally pictures of the
times they describe. He is himself saturated with the litera-
ture and history of the period, and what mainly distinguishes
his books is the fact that they are in considerable part made
up of contemporary letters and memoirs, so that the reader
hears the characters themselves speak, and is brought into
the closest imaginary contact with them. Moreover, the
complexion of the mosaic thus cleverly mortised is familiar
rather than heroic. The historian is not above gossip in
its good sense, and the way in which the life of the time
and of its distinguished personages is depicted is extremely
intimate as well as vivid and truthful.

The ten volumes now issued and in press relate to Marie
Antoinette, Josephine and Marie Louise. They give a vivid
representation of the momentous times immediately before,
during and after the epoch of the Revolution. Probably no
times in any country were ever so picturesque, so crowded
with events, and so peopled with striking characters. The
characteristics of the old régime and the events of the early

years of the Revolution are grouped effectively around the sympathetic figure of Louis Sixteenth's queen. In the first two books in which she figures, Josephine is taken as the center of the new society that issued from the disorganization wrought by the Revolution, and the third describes the beginning of the Imperial epoch. In "The Happy Days of the Empress Marie Louise," we are led behind the scenes, and shown the domestic life as well as the splendid court pomp of the world's Conqueror at the acme of his career—a most dramatic contrast with the picture drawn in the concluding three volumes, which describe the "Decadence of the Empire" owing to the Russian campaign, the "Invasion of 1814" and the "Return from Elba and the Hundred Days."

FAMOUS WOMEN OF THE FRENCH COURT.

FROM THE FRENCH OF IMBERT DE SAINT-AMAND.

Each with Portrait, 12mo, $1.25.

THREE VOLUMES ON MARIE ANTOINETTE.

MARIE ANTOINETTE AND THE END OF THE OLD RÉGIME.
MARIE ANTOINETTE AT THE TUILERIES.
MARIE ANTOINETTE AND THE DOWNFALL OF ROYALTY.

THREE VOLUMES ON THE EMPRESS JOSEPHINE.

CITIZENESS BONAPARTE.
THE WIFE OF THE FIRST CONSUL.
THE COURT OF THE EMPRESS JOSEPHINE.

FOUR VOLUMES ON THE EMPRESS MARIE LOUISE.

THE HAPPY DAYS OF MARIE LOUISE.
MARIE LOUISE AND THE DECADENCE OF THE EMPIRE.
MARIE LOUISE AND THE INVASION OF 1814.
MARIE LOUISE, THE RETURN FROM ELBA AND THE HUNDRED DAYS.

"In these translations of this interesting series of sketches, we have found an unexpected amount of pleasure and profit. The author cites for us passages from forgotten diaries, hitherto unearthed letters, extracts from public proceedings, and the like, and contrives to combine and arrange his material so as to make a great many very vivid and pleasing pictures. Nor is this all. The material he lays before us is of real value, and much, if not most of it, must be unknown save to the special students of the period. We can, therefore, cordially commend these books to the attention of our readers. They will find them attractive in their arrangement, never dull, with much variety of scene and incident, and admirably translated."—THE NATION, *of December 19, 1890.*

Marie Antoinette and the End of the Old Régime.

The years immediately preceding the outbreak of the Revolution comprise the epoch treated under this title, which aptly characterizes the passing away of the old order, before the tremendous social as well as political upheaval of the Revolution.

Marie Antoinette at the Tuileries.

The vicissitudes of the Royal Family, and incidentally the political history of the time, from the forcible removal from Versailles in 1789 to the end of 1791, including the unfortunate attempt at flight and the arrest at Varennes are the subject of this book.

Marie Antoinette and the Downfall of Royalty.

Continuing the story of the preceding volume, the author here narrates the turbulent and terrible scenes of the beginning of the Terror and closes with the abolition of royalty, the declaration of the Republic and the confinement of the Royal Family in the Temple.

Citizeness Bonaparte.

The period during which Josephine was called "Citizeness Bonaparte" is the romantic and eventful one beginning with her marriage, comprising the first Italian campaign and the Egyptian Expedition, and ending with the *coup d'état* of Brumaire.

The Wife of the First Consul.

As wife of the First Consul, Josephine presided over the brilliant society which issued from the social chaos of the Revolution and which, together with striking portraits of its principal figures, is here vividly described.

The Court of the Empress Josephine.

The events which took place between the assumption by Napoleon of the imperial title and the end of 1807, including the magnificent coronation ceremonies at Paris and at Milan and the wonderful campaign of Austerlitz are here described, as well as the daily life and surroundings of Josephine at the summit of her career.

The Happy Days of the Empress Marie Louise.

The happiest part of Marie Louise's career as Empress of the French, dating from her marriage, the festivities of which were celebrated with unexampled splendor, to the departure of the Grand Army for the disastrous Russian campaign, is the subject of this book.

Marie Louise and the Decadence of the Empire.

The period covered in this volume is the intensely dramatic decline of the French empire from the Russian campaign, when Marie Louise "had the world at her feet," to the desperate campaign of 1814 which concluded her brief but brilliant reign.

Marie Louise and the Invasion of 1814.

This volume takes the reader from the beginning of 1814 to Napoleon's second abdication and departure for Elba. In a military point of view this campaign, his first fought on French soil and resulting in his downfall and that of his dynasty, ranks, nevertheless, among his ablest, and the narrative of it is, perhaps, the most intensely interesting, the variations of fortune being so rapid and so momentous.

Marie Louise, the Return from Elba and the Hundred Days.

The final scenes of the Napoleonic drama are here unfolded—the imprisoned conqueror's life at Elba, his romantic escape and return to France, his almost miraculous resumption of power, the preparations for the last struggle and the climax of Waterloo and the definite restoration of Louis XVIII, closing the era begun in 1789.

CRITICAL NOTICES.

" A delightfully gossippy series."—*Philadelphia Press.*

" This volume [' Marie Louise and the Decadence of the Empire'] is as fascinating as any in the series, and the whole can be read with great profit and enjoyment."—*Hartford Courant.*

"Readers of the author's preceding volumes will not need to be told that the present one is full of charm and interest, brilliant description, and strong and clear historical sketches."—*New York Tribune.*

"The volumes are even more pictures of the times than of the unhappy occupants of the French throne. The style is clear and familiar, and the smaller courts of the period, the gossip of the court and the course of history, give interest other than biographical to the work."—*Baltimore Sun.*

" M. de Saint-Amand makes the great personages of whom he writes very human. In this last volume he has brought to light much new material regarding the diplomatic relations between Napoleon and the Austrian court, and throughout the series he presents, with a wealth of detail, the ceremonious and private life of the courts."—*San Francisco Argonaut.*

" The sketches, like the times to which they relate, are immensely dramatic. M. Saint-Amand writes with a vivid pen. He has filled himself with the history and the life of the times, and possesses the art of making them live in his pages. His books are capital reading, and remain as vivacious as idiomatic, and as pointed in the translation as in the original French."—*The Independent.*

" The last volume of the highly interesting series is characterized by all that remarkable attractiveness of description, historical and personal, that has made the former volumes of the series so popular. M. de Saint-Amand's pictures of court life and of the brilliant men and women that composed it, make the whole read with a freshness that is as fascinating as it is instructive."—*Boston Home Journal.*

" M. de Saint-Amand's volumes are inspired with such brightness, knowledge, and appreciation, that their value as studies in a great historical epoch requires acknowledgement. Though written mainly to entertain in a wholesome way, they also instruct the reader and give him larger views. That they have not before been translated for publication here is a little singular. Now, that their time has come, people should receive them gratefully while they read them with the attention they invite and deserve."—*N. Y. Times.*

"These volumes give animated pictures, romantic in coloring, intimate in detail, and entertaining from beginning to end. To the student of history they furnish the more charming details of gossip and court life which he has not found in his musty tomes ; while in the novice they must be the lode-stone leading to more minute research. The series is of more than transient value in that it teaches the facts of history through the medium of anecdote, description, and pen portraits ; this treatment having none of the dryness of history *per se*, but rather the brilliancy of romance."—*Boston Times.*

" The central figure of the lovely Josephine attracts sympathy and admiration as does hardly one other historical character. We have abundance of gossip of the less harmful kind, spirited portraits of men and women of note, glimpses here and there of the under-current of ambition and anxiety that lay beneath the brilliant court life, anecdotes in abundance, and altogether a bustling, animated, splendidly shifting panorama of life in the First Empire. No such revelation of the private life of Napoleon and Josephine has hitherto been given to the world as in 'The Court of the Empress Josephine.' It is the author's masterpiece."—*Christian Union.*

www.ingramcontent.com/pod-product-compliance
Lightning Source LLC
Chambersburg PA
CBHW031227090426
42740CB00007B/741